Cross-National Appropriation of Work Systems

Cross-National Appropriation of Work Systems

Japanese Firms in the UK

Ayse Saka

Research Fellow in International Economics and Business, University of Groningen, The Netherlands

Edward Elgar

Cheltenham, UK • Northampton, MA, USA

Published by
Edward Elgar Publishing Limited
Glensanda House
Montpellier Parade
Cheltenham
Glos GL50 1UA
UK

Edward Elgar Publishing, Inc.
136 West Street
Suite 202
Northampton
Massachusetts 01060
USA

A catalogue record for this book
is available from the British Library

Library of Congress Cataloguing in Publication Data
Saka, Ayse, 1972–
    Cross-national appropriation of work systems : Japanese firms in the UK / Ayse Saka.
        p. cm.
    Includes bibliographical references and index.
    1. Investments, Japanese—Great Britain. 2. Technology transfer—Great Britain. 3. Diffusion of innovation—Great Britain. I. Title.

HG5432.S24 2003
338.6'0941—dc21   2003049037

ISBN 1 84376 112 2

Printed and bound in Great Britain by MPG Books Ltd, Bodmin, Cornwall

Contents

Figures

Tables

Preface

The study of cross-national diffusion of production systems has a certain tradition. We know a lot about how carefully designed programmes of change that focus primarily on the conditions for the 'successful' diffusion of production systems affect local or national management and industrial relations. We have come to understand that parts of the effect, notably in Britain, may be due to a more general 'greenfield site' effect, that is to say the fact that the plant can be built up anew from scratch, and the focus on diffusing explicit, as opposed to tacit, elements of production systems.

The present study, which has been conducted in order to obtain a PhD at Warwick Business School, continues this line of inquiry. It is particularly geared to decompose effects by comparing greenfield with brownfield foreign direct investments and alliance formations. It therefore shows us results which had been anticipated, more clearly on the basis of a two-step comparative historical analysis. But this is not all, and maybe not the most important message which comes out. For it calls into question the conceptual slant which has undergirded much previous research, by inquiring into effects of transfer, of initially Japanese practices. What we now see is that 'transfer' is not really an appropriate notion. For what we witness, the author tells us, is translation rather than transfer. Transfer evokes a more passive or submissive stance whilst translation brackets the more active interpretation, adaptation and implementation of recipes. In this manner, the study reminds us, lest we forget at a time when superficial slogans like globalization or 'global village' are bandied about, that local practice always has an inventive side to it and points to the continuation or invention of local specificities, even if that practice is dependent on much more general concepts and levels of governance.

I would also recommend this study in a more general way, beyond the specific topic and its disciplinary ambit, for the combination of methodological rigour with qualitative sensitivity in interviewing and analysis. This shows what theoretically meaningful research in the more qualitative veneer, beyond genuflections towards Ragin or Eisenstadt, looks like.

Arndt Sorge
Groningen, October 2002

Acknowledgements

There are quite a number of people who have contributed to the development and completion of the doctoral study on which this book is based. 1 extend my cordial gratitude to the following people.

I am grateful to Professor Jacky Swan and Mr. Glenn Morgan for their invaluable guidance as supervisors in bringing this research to a rewarding conclusion. They have not only extended their constructive critical comments on the work in progress of the doctoral study but also provided moral support in other aspects of academic life. I appreciate the viva environment of fair professional inquiry created by my external examiner, Professor Ray Loveridge, and internal examiner, Dr. Diana Sharpe.

This work would not have come to light without the access provided by the companies investigated. I am thankful to Mr. Bryan McGinity, the MD of Teniki UK, and Toshiya Tsutsumi-san for arranging my interviews at Teniki in Japan, as well as showing genuine interest and support in a context of sincere friendship throughout the study.

My gratitude is also extended to Chris Melbourne who arranged for my week-long work experience on the shop floor of Nissera UK, Shigeru Nirasawa-san for arranging my interviews at Nissera in Japan and Atsuo Nagai-san, the President of Nissera, for his cherishable hospitality during my visit to Nissera.

It was a pleasure for me to gain the insights of the electrical engineers at Rover through Ray Gibbard's assistance. Rover members' contributions to this study, in particular those of Malcolm Caston, Dave Rose and Adrian Smith, are immense. They have been very patient in responding to my never-ending list of questions. I must especially note Dave Rose's forbearance in coping with my constant requests for feedback. He has served as a bridge between the academic and business world by sensitizing me to the practical concerns of the automotive world. I am also indebted to Shuko Hayashi-san, whom I met through Peter McVeigh and John Bacchus at Rover, and Kenzo Suzuki-san for supporting my visit to Honda Motor Corporation and Tochigi R&D Centre of Honda in Japan. Kenzo Suzuki-san, the Executive Vice-President of Honda R&D Europe at the time of this research, has helped me contextualize the Japanese perspective on my research topic by introducing me to the delicacy of the Japanese culture.

I must also thank the participants of the European Summer Research Institutes (ESRI) PhD Summer School on Comparative Study of Economic Organization organized by Copenhagen Business School in September 1999 for shaping my preliminary ideas, as well as those of the sub-theme convened by Professor Marie-Laure Djelic and Dr. Sigrid Quack at the 16th European Group for Organization Studies (EGOS) Colloquium in July 2000 in Helsinki for their detailed suggestions for the refinement and fine-tuning of my arguments.

My close friends – Chia Hsuan (Grace) Kuan, who has been a supporting pillar in my trough periods and Izumi Kubo, who has exposed me to the Japanese mode of thinking through her anecdotes and has hosted me in Tokyo during my data collection in Japan – have been a source of emotional strength.

The unflagging encouragement and confidence of my parents, Mehmet Polat and Gülten Saka, and two sisters, Banu and Çiğdem, have been an impetus in completing this research. The unconditional care and understanding they have shown me during the process can never be reciprocated.

Last but not least, I would like to thank Muğla University in Turkey for providing me with financial support for the research.

PART I

Theoretical background

Introduction

This book investigates the influence of national and local institutional variation on the internalization of work systems. It focuses on the degree to which strongly institutionalized organizational practices that are driven by people's knowledge, ideas and suggestions can be diffused to a less densely institutionalized environment. The aim is to reflect the active process of internalizing that goes with implementing work systems, as well as to highlight the structural limits to accepting alternative work systems.

1. BACKGROUND

There is a growing body of literature on work systems diffusion (for example Richter and Vettel, 1995; Mowery et al., 1996). Researchers have adopted a comparative research approach to work systems diffusion from a variety of angles such as the following: the labour process and lean production perspectives within the Japanization literature (for example Stewart, 1998; Womack et al., 1990 respectively), the user-oriented perspective in the innovation processes literature (for example Scarbrough et al., 1998) and the historical neo-institutional perspective within the neo-institutional literature (for example Whitley, 1999b). However, there are marked differences across these perspectives with regard to: (i) a processual or structural/technical focus; (ii) an intra-firm or inter-firm level of investigation; (iii) a reference to universal or embedded framework and (iv) the objective or context-dependent view of work systems diffusion. This book adopts the historical neo-institutional perspective to highlight the institutional limits to the diffusion of work systems across nations. Few attempts have been made to shed light upon the difficulties in implementing alternative work systems in cross-national settings. Although attention is paid to the influence of institutional characteristics on the extent to which work systems are diffused within the innovation processes literature (for example Swan et al., 1999), this has not provided a systematic comparison of the context-bound nature of work systems diffusion. The focus has been on internal processes of innovation design particularly within 'knowledge-intensive' firms. The study reported here extends the discussion on knowledge to a new empirical context – the shop floor of a car component manufacturer. Attention to the

3

internalization of alternative work systems by factory operators has essentially been disregarded by researchers operating in the innovation processes literature. Rather, scholars have tended to limit their investigations to sector-specific knowledge diffusion processes in consultancies, software companies and innovation centres (for example Lahti and Beyerlein, 2000). Their focus has been on the process of diffusing organizational structures and processes, including HRM activities.

Research on work systems diffusion commonly adopts the objectified view of diffusion processes that reflects the interest in tangible characteristics such as structure and technology. This is illustrated by economic accounts of work systems diffusion within multinational operations (for example Marton, 1986; Prahalad and Hamel, 1990; Kogut and Zander, 1992; Bresman et al., 1999). There is an attempt in such studies to link knowledge to a performance outcome (for example Leonard-Barton, 1995; Makino and Delios, 1996). In this sense, the firm is treated as a repository of capabilities or competences, and knowledge is seen as an objectified commodity (for example Barney, 1991; Fransman, 1994; Teece and Pisano, 1994). The limits to diffusion and embeddedness of work systems in institutional settings are not acknowledged.

Although a number of comparative studies have shown variation in the internalization of work systems across different capitalist systems (for example Sako, 1992; Lane, 1996), evidence from these studies is confined to the macro level. The dynamics of how diffused work systems are shaped within the firm have received less attention. Clark's (1987) work on macro-to micro-level analysis of the way 'work templates' are appropriated is one of the few exceptions. An attempt is made in this book to complement the national-level discussions with the organizational level by providing an analysis of the social patterns that shape the internalization process.

2.   RESEARCH OBJECTIVES

The book aims to reflect the active process of internalizing that goes with implementing work systems. When work systems are highly localized in character and acquired through engagement in specific action contexts, they can prove to be 'sticky' to diffuse to foreign firms (Szulanski, 1996). This is especially the case in Japan, where the activities of 'highly co-ordinated' business system (Whitley, 1999b) are generally carried out in accordance with highly implicit rules and social norms. 'Compromise' (Sharpe, 1997) or 'hybrid' (Abo, 1994) solutions are common where Japanese belief systems, which are not readily compatible with those of the adopter firm, are diffused to 'foreign' contexts (for example Besser, 1996; Mair, 1998). Work systems are seen here as embedded at two levels: in the form of institutional embed-dedness at the national level and tacit embeddedness at the organizational level. Embeddedness, which reflects behaviour that is aimed at sociability, approval, status and power, incorporates the impact of social structure and social relations on production, distribution or consumption (Granovetter, 1985). In this book, macro-level embeddedness addresses the nationally dis-tinct characteristics of social institutions, such as legitimacy of Japanese and UK business systems, including structural characteristics of organizations and human resource management (HRM) systems. Micro-level embedded-ness addresses the difficulty in the diffusion of work systems owing to the tacit nature of Japanese work systems.

The empirical evidence highlights the extent to which structural (partici-pation through teams, shift in authority relations), cultural (values and norms that constitute the philosophies which underlie the structural and technical elements of continuous improvement schemes), control-related (perceived exercise of power) and technological (advanced production systems technology that is needed for the efficient running of technical systems) practices are accepted and put to use by UK adopter firms. This is accomplished by examining the nature of the influence of local institu-tional (such as location site and skills base of labour) and organizational (such as company size and age, as well as employee attitude towards alter-native work systems) characteristics on work systems diffusion. The insti-tutional and organizational levels are addressed in an effort to consider the contextual embeddedness of work systems, as well as to attain theoretical saturation and a robust explanation through comparative study.

With regard to the aim of the study, the central question may be formu-lated as follows:

> What is the impact of national and local institutional variation on the diffusion of work systems in multinational corporations' internationalization efforts?

This question can be subdivided into theoretical and empirical questions:

At the theoretical level:

- What are the key attributes of work systems diffusion?
- Which characteristics at local institutional and organizational levels are likely to have an impact on the diffusability of work systems across nations?

At the empirical level:

- Which characteristics are likely to either hinder or facilitate affiliate firms' adoption of multinational corporations' work systems?

The answers to the first two theoretical questions are drawn from the literature and form the building blocks of the analytic schema. This schema guides the field study and the subsequent analysis, which are intended to provide the answer to the empirical question.

3.   RESEARCH DESIGN

The research on which this book is based adopts a comparative approach to investigating the ways in which Japanese work systems are adopted and sustained in affiliate firms of Japanese multinational corporations (MNCs) in the UK automotive manufacture sector. The process of diffusing work systems forms the central unit of analysis. The study looks at underlying processes (for example Sharpe, 1999), not only structures (for example Abo, 1994). This enables ongoing processes to be examined in a non-static manner. It is assumed here that an investigation of processes can reveal a set of meanings attached to work systems that is interwoven with structure and technology. The challenge here is to understand both the structural aspects and the subjective meanings attached to them. Moreover, the diffusion process is largely investigated from the adopter company's perspective, as it is felt that 'diffusion begins not with the sender but with what Rogers[1] terms the adopter' (Cutcher-Gershenfeld et al., 1998, p. 42).

Qualitative case studies, which draw on semi-structured interviews, participant observation, factory tours and document analysis, are conducted in the UK subsidiary firms of Japanese MNCs (a brownfield and a greenfield site) and an Anglo-Japanese technical collaboration. The aim here is to observe the degree to which institutional variation between Japan and the UK influences the internalization of Japanese work systems in the UK. The two countries in the study are seen as constituting contrasting institutional settings (see Whitley, 1999b). The fundamental line of reasoning underlying this study is that institutional and organizational characteristics can hinder or facilitate the degree to which the source company's work systems may be internalized by adopter firms (see Figure I.1).

In the schema in Figure I.1, which will be further developed in Chapter One, the implementation and internalization of work systems, which are seen here as components of the diffusion process, form the central unit of analysis. The degree of internalization by employees at adopter firms can be explained by linking it to the nature of institutional and organizational characteristics. The two-level characteristics that are considered particularly relevant in this respect are drawn from the literature and labelled here as key characteristics.

Bearing in mind the aim of the study, the sampled cases need to contain

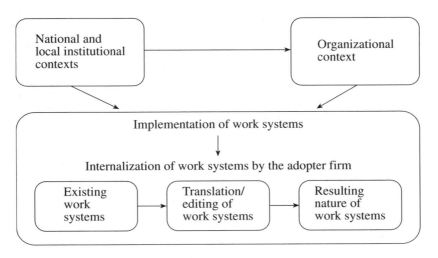

Figure I.1   Schema for the diffusion of work systems

detailed descriptions of the extent to which work systems are diffused and the nature of social institutions at the national and local levels in the automotive manufacture sector. In this way, key institutional and organizational characteristics that can influence the degree of implementation and internalization of alternative work systems may be identified.

The empirical setting of this study is the automotive manufacturing sector. It represents an important industry from the standpoint of national competitiveness. The number of Japanese manufacturers in Europe increased by 16 during 1997 to a total of 859, with the UK retaining its lead (247 manufacturers, 20 per cent of the EU total) over the rest of the EU. The UK also had the highest number of new investments during 1997. 'There were 362 at end-1997, of which the UK hosted 127 (35 per cent), Germany 66 and France 50' (News and Notes section of *Euro-Japanese Journal*, 1999: 59). It is claimed that 'the adoption of the latest working [in the UK] has resulted in a revolution in manufacturing skills and performance' (Invest in Britain Bureau, 1999, which is currently known as Invest UK). Furthermore, the quality and productivity of the output from UK factories is said to rival the best in the world – including Japan – owing to the diffusion of 'lean manufacturing' systems and commitment to continuous improvement. The selection of the automotive manufacturing sector allows one to investigate the possible limits to the adoption of Japanese work systems due to the heavy emphasis on the transfer of the 'Japanese' model in this sector. The number of Japanese investments is greater within the automotive sector than it is in other sectors such as semiconductors; chemical, plastic,

*Table I.1   Japanese foreign direct investment in the UK by product
              category*

Sector	Number of companies
Semiconductors related industry	4 (2%)
Automobile and automobile parts	35 (15%)
Machinery and engineering	34 (14.5%)
Chemical, plastics, pharmaceutical and healthcare	27 (11.5%)
Textiles and apparel	17 (7%)
Food and drinks	8 (3%)
Electrical and precision, machinery, office automation equipment, information and communication industry and components	93 (40%)
Others	16 (7%)
Total	234

Source: Invest in Britain Bureau (1995), currently Invest UK

pharmaceutical and healthcare; textile and apparel; and food and drinks
(see Table I.1).

Although the literature on Japanization provides an extensive study of
the automotive sector, it does not sufficiently explain the social process of
work systems diffusion and the way artefacts are understood by human
actors. Whilst the study of patterns of knowing as a dynamic activity is
better addressed by the innovation processes literature, a large number of
studies in this field do not address the impact of macro-institutional structures on work systems diffusion in a particular industry, but rather focuses
on human or technical processes underlying technology diffusion at a
project or a national level (for example Clark, 1987). This study emphasizes
the diffusion of work systems within production-related operations. It
adopts the historical neo-institutional perspective to link characteristics of
work systems to path dependencies within particular institutional settings.

4.   ORGANIZATION OF THE BOOK

The book consists of five chapters. Chapter One provides a closer exami-
nation of the concepts of work systems, work systems diffusion and their
embeddedness at the national and organizational levels. The book is posi-
tioned with respect to different perspectives on comparative research
approaches to work systems diffusion, specifically the labour process and

'lean production' perspectives within the 'Japanization' literature, the user-oriented perspective within the innovation processes literature and the historical neo-institutional perspective grounded in the neo-institutional literature. The institutional embeddedness of actors is discussed with particular emphasis on Whitley's divergent capitalisms argument within the historical neo-institutional perspective. Further in Chapter One, an analytic framework is provided for a systematic comparison of the process of work systems diffusion across three affiliate firms of Japanese MNCs in the UK. This is followed, in Chapter Two, by a discussion of the analytic framework with reference to the diversity of capitalist systems and emphasis on different types of knowledge in Japan and the UK. This discussion is reflected in five propositions. Chapter Three presents the methodological aspects of the empirical study. The case studies conducted in the UK affiliate firms of Japanese multinationals in the automotive sector that serve to illustrate the institutional limits to the diffusion of work systems are detailed in Chapter Four. The results of the analysis are compared with the analytic framework developed in Chapter One and the propositions formulated in Chapter Two. Finally, in Chapter Five, the study outcomes are used to highlight the central role of appropriation in diffusion, and the theoretical and practical implications as well as the limitations of the research findings are discussed.

NOTES

1.   The authors refer to Rogers' (1983) work, entitled *Diffusion of Innovations*, Third edition. New York: Free Press.

1. Work systems diffusion: neo-institutional perspectives

1. INTRODUCTION

This chapter provides a review of the concepts of work systems and work systems diffusion. Work systems are seen as embedded at two levels: in the form of, first, institutional embeddedness at national level, and second, embeddedness of tacit work systems at organizational level. The chapter provides a working definition of the diffusion of work systems at organizational level with reference to the view of work systems as knowledge-driven. This is supplemented by a review of comparative research approaches to work systems diffusion. These are specifically perspectives in the 'Japanization', innovation processes and neo-institutional literatures. The four major perspectives on work systems diffusion are reviewed in an attempt to situate the conceptual framework within an appropriate theoretical perspective. On the basis of this review, the neo-institutional arguments on the diffusion of work systems are identified as providing the most appropriate conceptual foundation for the construction of an analytic framework. Two different perspectives within the neo-institutional literature (the rational choice and historical neo-institutional perspectives) are highlighted. The neo-institutional framework is further developed by strengthening it with concepts from the innovation processes literature. An analytic framework is constructed to offer a set of concepts that can provide answers to the following two questions. First, what are the key attributes of work systems? Second, what characteristics at the local institutional and organizational levels are likely to have an impact on the diffusion of work systems across nations?

2. DIFFUSION OF WORK SYSTEMS

Working Definition of Work Systems

According to Whitley (1999c), work systems are distinctive interrelated patterns of task organization and control, workplace relations between social groups, and employment practices and policies. This study focuses on work systems that are essentially organizational practices, which are dependent on continuous improvement in operations. It highlights work systems as driven by people's knowledge, ideas and suggestions and as 'premised on harnessing the knowledge at the point where products are made or services are delivered' (Cutcher-Gershenfeld et al., 1998, p. 69). Bearing this definition in mind, work systems are referred to here as knowledge-driven. It is not the purpose of this book to draw an analytic distinction between work systems that are knowledge-driven and those that are not. On the contrary, the study aims to acknowledge the knowledge-driven nature of all work systems. Nonetheless, it should be noted that tacit work systems, such as those emphasized by Japanese firms, are argued here to be driven by people's knowledge, ideas and suggestions to a greater degree than explicit or decontextualized work systems, such as those reflected by Anglo-Saxon operations (see Chapter Two for further discussion).

This study aims to examine the introduction of alternative work systems across cultures, and sees these as key to global business strategy. Although the diffusion of knowledge-driven work systems can be investigated in any empirical context,[1] the focus in this book is on knowledge diffusion on the shop floor and in an engineering project. The basic premise is that knowledge diffusion occurs with equal importance on the shop floor and in engineering projects as it does in research and development (R&D) centres and knowledge-intensive firms such as software development and consultancy firms. Hence, the capabilities of 'ordinary' factories and engineering firms are seen in terms of 'knowledge works' (Fruin, 1997). Prusak (1997) notes that as products are increasingly 'smart', production processes need to process higher levels of information about changing customer requirements and delivery times. Hence, knowledge production and diffusion apply right across the board.

Discussions on the diffusion of work systems within the manufacturing context have commonly centred on structural and technical issues such as the cost and quality advantages of reduced inventory and efficiency gains from concurrent engineering.[2] The definition adopted here diverges from privileging organizational structures and technological systems as the driving forces of work systems diffusion. Rather, it emphasizes the importance of intangible aspects, in addition to acknowledging the tangibles. Hence, this book adopts a more processual view on the diffusion of work systems. Cutcher-Gershenfeld et al. (1998, p. 10) argue that the diffusion of intangible capabilities, much more than the tangible work practices or technical/structural systems, represents the key source of competitive advantage. Such diffusion marks the importance given to people at all levels of the organization who must combine 'the mastery of some highly specialized technical expertise with the ability to work effectively in teams, form productive relationships with clients and critically reflect on and then change their own organizational practices' (Argyris, 1991: 100).

The definition of work systems as knowledge-driven reflects a socio-technical perspective in which human interaction at all levels of the firm is seen as being as vital as technology itself. In addition to acknowledging the technical and structural aspects of work systems, this definition gives allegiance to human beings as actively discovering problems and creating knowledge to solve them. Hence, work systems are envisaged as incorporating the management of people (see Takeuchi, 1998). Bird et al. (1999) assert that the importance of the human factor in the value-added activities of the firm rises as national barriers to the flow of capital and technology fall. The importance of an effective management of human resources is recognized especially in the context of Japanese firms, which are seen as relying more extensively on people-oriented work systems as a means of achieving competitive advantage (Abo, 1994).

Objectified and Context-Dependent Views of Work Systems Diffusion

The traditional view of work systems diffusion reflects the interest in technology that is commonly taken as the primary source of competitive advantage. However, a complex set of meanings attached to work systems urges one to investigate the ways in which structure and technology are interwoven in organizational practice. At one extreme, that is in part reflected by the information technology- and knowledge management-driven arguments, researchers have argued for technological determinism within a contingency framework. In other words, particular kinds of technology are proposed to yield certain predictable outcomes (see Womack et al., 1990). This extreme constitutes the more linear, mechanistic view of diffusion, where work systems (with an emphasis on explicit features) are seen as imported from or adopted out of a 'foreign' context in a unitary fashion. In other words, work systems are 'black-boxed' as technological artefacts and 'transferred'. This stream of research reflects Wolfe's (1994) category of 'organizational innovativeness' in his review of the innovation literature. He argues that there is a tendency to focus on the structural variables as the primary determinants of innovation. This static orientation ignores 'changes in an innovation during the innovation process' (ibid.: 409).

Studies have been carried out outside the manufacturing setting on work systems diffusion in high-tech firms, such as software development (for example Lahti and Beyerlein, 2000), labelled as 'knowledge-intensive firms' (Tampoe, 1993). This is mainly derived from the association of knowledge with technology, where technology diffusion is seen as synonymous with knowledge diffusion (for example Lynskey, 1999). Other researchers have challenged the dichotomy between technology and people. They have addressed the 'sharp decrease in attention to people management and development issues, and step increase in attention to information technology (IT), information systems (IS) and intellectual capital' (Swan, 1999, p. 4), seeing technological and structural characteristics of work systems as embedded in a social set of norms and beliefs (Thomas, 1994). The importance of their view is reflected in part by the process theory research on organization innovation (Wolfe, 1994). This research investigates 'the nature of the innovation process, how and why innovations emerge, develop, grow and (perhaps) terminate' (ibid.: 409). In brief, of the two perspectives, one emphasizes the technical aspects of work systems and regards the diffusion of knowledge-driven work systems as objectified, and the other focuses on the social aspects and sees the diffusion of knowledge-driven work systems as context-dependent.

The two perspectives emphasize different aspects of the knowledge diffusion process. The perspective that pays heed to the context-dependent nature of knowledge-driven work systems diffusion emphasizes 'culture management and leadership as a means for encouraging both socialization, so that tacit knowledge is shared, and also internalization of explicit knowledge into the values and tacit understandings of employees' (Scarbrough et al., 1998, p. 39). This perspective reflects the sedimented mode of knowledge communication 'where knowledge is communicated via rules, standards, routines and structures' (Scarbrough, 1995: 999). Actors can develop strategies that involve the progressive delimiting and fixing of social relations. The meaning of alternative work systems becomes progressively stabilized as users and producers come to share common frameworks as to the meaning, critical features and purpose of the diffused systems. The context-dependent view of work systems diffusion focuses on 'knowledge communication through professionalism and an intensively cultivated employment relationship which [seeks] to bind individuals tightly to the organization' (ibid.: 1012). This view acknowledges the stickiness of knowledge-driven work systems and, in turn, the limitations to diffusion across institutional contexts. (This is exemplified in Chapter Two.) In contrast, the objectified view of knowledge-driven work systems diffusion implies that practices can easily be transplanted to a new institutional setting. The diffusion process is generally analysed through broadcasting analogies. Scarbrough (1995) refers to this process as communicating knowledge through objectification or universal applicability through standardization. This process requires that technical knowledge be separated from its social context by standardization and segmentation.

This book builds on the perspective that takes into account the context-sensitive nature of knowledge-driven work systems. It attempts to provide insights into the social constitution of work systems by highlighting the inter-related aspects of technical and structural systems (in other words, largely the tangibles), and people, training, discipline, management–worker relations and social networks (in other words, largely the intangibles) in a process. Work systems are seen as embedded in a wider social context. For example, the quality circle in Japan is embedded in a set of cultural assumptions about hands-on management and employment security, as well as internal labour market structure. Interactions of multiple actors shape the diffusion of work systems. In the words of Cutcher-Gershenfeld et al. (1998, p. 11), the diffusion of work systems is seen as 'a highly complex, negotiated process put into operation in a diverse range of communities and workforces'.

Knowledge-driven work systems, rooted as they are in firms' coordina-tion mechanisms and organizational routines, exist in tacit and explicit form (Polanyi, 1966; Senker, 1995). They incorporate the cognitive dimen-sion, that is beliefs, perceptions, ideals, values, emotions and mental models that are taken for granted (Takeuchi, 1998). Particular means of solving problems, carrying out tasks and arriving at decisions become institution-alized over time with the influence of past and present actions, beliefs and interests (Clark and Mueller, 1994). This has implications for a firm's ability to create core organizational capabilities that rest on a combination of what Araujo (1998: 320) calls migratory 'lower-level' skills and 'higher-order', that is less diffusable, routines.

The complementary tacit and explicit forms of work systems are not sharply divided. While tacit knowledge can be possessed by itself, explicit knowledge must rely on being tacitly understood and applied. Hence, 'all knowledge is either tacit or rooted in tacit knowledge' (Polanyi, 1966, p. 144). Tacit work systems are taken to reflect organizational routines that have been standardized over time to assume a taken-for-granted, subcon-scious nature (Kostova, 1999). In other words, tacit knowledge is taken as experiential, practical knowledge that is embedded in habit, skills, routine, practices and/or teamwork (Polanyi, op. cit.). It is believed to be effectively diffused through personnel transfers and visits (Inkpen and Dinur, 1998; Bresman et al., 1999). Tacit knowledge is operationalized here as the *intan-gible* foundation of continuous improvement schemes, whereas explicit knowledge is defined independently of a particular individual or a group, and is regarded as being transmitted by 'book, blueprint or statement to everyone on equal terms' (Best, 1990, p. 127). It is operationalized here as the *tangible* foundation of continuous improvement schemes. For example, organizational structures as tangibles in a given process are generally abstracted from their contexts to reflect explicit forms of knowledge.

The distinction between tacit and explicit forms may also be observed in the classification of scientific and practical knowledge of 'time and place'

(Hayek, 1945), 'objective and experiential' knowledge (Penrose, 1959), 'migratory and embedded' knowledge (Badaracco, 1991), and 'idiosyncratic and codified' knowledge (Lanzara and Patriotta, 2000). This distinction is reflected in some of the definitions of information, which is associated with explicit knowledge, and know-how, which is related to tacit knowledge. For example, information is defined by Dyer and Nobeoka (2000: 348, brackets added) as 'easily codifiable [or explicit] knowledge that can be transmitted without loss of integrity once the syntactical rules required for deciphering it are known . . . by comparison, know-how [or tacit knowledge] involves knowledge that is tacit, "sticky", complex, and difficult to codify'. Consequently, knowledge ingrained in highly tacit work systems can prove to be 'sticky' (Szulanski, 1996) to diffuse to 'foreign' firms. Such knowledge can lack the tacit embedding context of its home country. More often than not 'what makes sense in one context can change or even lose its meaning when communicated to people in a different context' (Takeuchi, 1998: 8).

The distinction between tacit and explicit knowledge has been a focus of debate (for example Blackler, 1995; Tsoukas, 1996). Critics of this distinction argue that organizations are being portrayed as rich depositories of untapped knowledge which can be profitably exploited (for example Marshall and Sapsed, 2000). In line with Polanyi's (1966) argument, Tsoukas (op. cit.) regards tacit and explicit knowledge as mutually constituted, rather than as two separate types of knowledge. He contends that 'a firm's knowledge is distributed in the sense that it is inherently indeterminate' (ibid.: 22). Similarly, Blackler (1995: 1032) argues that 'knowledge is multifaceted and complex, being both situated and abstract, implicit and explicit, distributed and individual, physical and mental, developing and static, verbal and decoded.' Whilst acknowledging these debates, the present research, in line with other work (for example Nonaka and Takeuchi, 1995), makes a schematic distinction between tacit and explicit knowledge in order to frame and investigate the impact of the variation in the emphasis on different types of knowledge on the diffusion process. (The variation in emphasis is discussed in the context of Japanese and UK business systems in Chapter Two.)

The attributes of work systems diffusion
The work systems diffusion process can be conceptualized as being composed of two stages: (i) implementation and (ii) internalization. As this book adopts a context-dependent definition of knowledge and emphasizes the adopter or user side, as opposed to the supply side, of knowledge-driven work systems diffusion, it is proposed here that a theoretical distinction is needed between the implementation and internalization process. This is to

acknowledge the role of actors in appropriating work systems (Clark, 1987). The 'blending and redesign of technical systems alongside changes in organizational practices and local context' is referred to here as the appropriation of work systems (Swan et al., 1999: 906; Swan and Clark, 1992). It is seen as the process of unpacking and reblending new ideas within existing contexts in order to develop firm-specific solutions (Clark and Staunton, 1989). It should be noted that supply-oriented models 'presume that the only problems worth considering are inside the user firm at the stage of implementation' (Clark et al., 1992: 71). By contrast, this study attempts to investigate the diffusability of meaning, value attached to work systems in addition to structural and technical elements. Where the original meaning of the source company's practices are difficult to diffuse, the existing work practices are likely to be redefined and restructured until eventually they become routine.

The concept of 'knowledge-driven work systems diffusion' is used intentionally here. It is distinguished from the concept of 'knowledge-driven work systems transfer' which refers to a communications model that emphasizes the flow of technical skills or technological capabilities from source to affiliate firms (for example Mowery et al., 1996). In a communications model, knowledge is treated as an object that is created, packaged and moved in an unchanged form from one unit to another (Hislop et al., 1998). By contrast, the concept of 'diffusion' explains 'how new ideas are communicated and why some ideas are chosen (or rejected)', or why so many ideas fail during implementation or generate unanticipated consequences (ibid.: 429). It points to sharing of knowledge across company lines, and is well suited to explaining the locally situated sense-making process of technical and organizational knowledge acquisition.

The introduction of 'new' work systems by management at the adopter firm is labelled here the 'implementation process' and is evident in formal mechanisms such as training programmes. The 'internalization process' refers to the routinization or institutionalization of work systems by workers and is evident in the attitudes of workers to diffused systems. More specifically, the internalization process refers to the acceptance and approval by employees of a practice that is infused with value (Kostova, 1999). For example, Abrahamson and Rosenkopf (1993: 492) argue that 'with increases in the number of organizations making independent problem-solving decisions to adopt an innovation, the innovation becomes increasingly "infused with value beyond the technical requirements of the task at hand" (Selznick, 1957, p. 17)'. In other words, many organizations adopt an innovation, based not on the individual organization's assessment of this innovation's efficiency or returns but on the fact that it is considered legitimate for organizations to use this innovation.

Comparative Research Approaches

Since the early 1980s, a number of approaches have emerged which allow the patterns observed in cross-national diffusion of work systems to be explained. These are, in particular the labour process view, which, broadly speaking, is a political as opposed to a technical perspective (Graham, 1993), and the lean production perspective within the 'Japanization' literature, the user-oriented perspective within the innovation processes literature and the historical neo-institutional perspective within the neo-institutional literature. In the next sections, the key features of these perspectives, including the issues on which they focus and the conceptual frameworks they offer, are discussed and compared in the light of the research aims. In this way, the most appropriate perspective is identified as the basis for the construction of the analytic framework that is used in this research.

The labour process perspective within the 'Japanization' literature

There is a growing body of literature (Morris, 1988; Oliver and Wilkinson, 1992; Stewart, 1998) addressing the issue of the diffusion of Japanese management systems through the globalization of Japanese manufacturers. Discussions have focused on issues of work and employment relations, labour control and effort intensification by management. Within the labour process perspective on the diffusion of Japanese work systems, the focus has mainly been on power and dependency implications of the diffusion process (Briggs, 1988; Dickens and Savage, 1988; Oliver et al., 1994; Skorstad, 1994; Danford, 1998; Delbridge, 1998). Workers are seen as detached from the means of production, and able to access them only by selling their labour to others (Braverman, 1998). The purpose of diffusing foreign work systems becomes 'the expansion of a unit of capital belonging to the employer, who is thus functioning as a capitalist' (ibid., p. 36). The Japanese work systems are seen as enabling management to enforce speedier methods and shortcuts to the manufacturing process in an attempt to dissociate the labour process from the skills of the workers. In other words, management prerogatives are celebrated to the detriment of the workforce (Oliver and Wilkinson, 1992). Attention is drawn to the introduction of Japanese systems through a selection process conducted according to the criteria and templates held by those who enjoy access to it. According to Westney (1999, p. 404), the criterion in this political view for diffusing organizational practices is to maintain parental control, or to enhance the power of the dominant coalition. Fundamentally, this approach highlights governance and control mechanisms implicit in the diffusion of Japanese work systems. For example, Sewell and Wilkinson (1992) argue that Japanese management exercises a covert form of social control or 'concertive control', to use

Barker's (1993) words. 'Concertive control', as opposed to 'bureaucratic rational control', is seen as growing out of a 'substantial consensus about values, high level co-ordination and a degree of self-management by members or workers in an organization' (ibid.: 408). This is achieved by giving employees the impression that they are empowered via quality circles and other team-based activities. Sewell and Wilkinson (1992: 271) demonstrate that the 'surveillance systems integral to JIT/TQM [just-in-time/total quality management] are deliberately designed such that discipline is established in a most efficient manner and the exercise of minute control is possible with a minimum of supervisors.' In Danford's (1997: 2) words, 'new management techniques secure for management new levers of control over skill deployment, task distribution and overall worker effort rates.' Furthermore, Oliver and Wilkinson (1992) discuss the social and political consequences of diffusing Japanese manufacturing methods. Their conceptualization of 'Japanization' is based on Ackroyd et al.'s (1988) definition of the term. Ackroyd et al. (ibid.) distinguish between direct, mediated, and permeated or full Japanization in considering its implication for British industry. Direct Japanization is taken to mean 'the penetration of British economy and industry by Japanese firms' (ibid.: 15). Deliberate or overt copying of Japanese policies or practices by British firms is referred to as mediated Japanization. In other words, the impact of the adoption of Japanese practices is not seen as a straightforward copying process, given that the effects of the practices are mediated by British management (ibid.).

Oliver and Wilkinson's (1992) arguments give voice to the barriers that the adopter firm faces in its efforts to sustain worker ownership of Japanese manufacturing techniques and philosophies. They also illustrate the selective character of any borrowing from Japan, where the given company seeks to adopt elements of the 'Japanese' model to match its circumstances. This results in the adoption of a hybrid which is neither entirely Japanese management as practised in Japan nor typically British (see Wilkinson and Oliver, 1992; see also White and Trevor, 1983). The 'selective' importation of organizations based on teamwork and devolved responsibility, extensive and intensive communication and employee relations systems is seen as designed to safeguard managerial prerogatives. The investment in trust-building, openness in communication and visibility in management by the Japanese are taken as a means of minimizing worker resistance and increasing the acceptance of a new governance system. This indirect form of control is seen as associated with a low willingness on the part of the Japanese companies to learn from their overseas affiliates, where the Japanese are in a strong bargaining position to establish ways of working they see as necessary (Smith and Elger, 1998). The Japanese firm's selective utilization of production practices that are identified with the 'Japanese model' (Taylor et al., 1994, p.197) suggests that practices of strategic importance, such as design work, remain in the Japanese headquarters. This ingrains the notion among critics that the Japanese managerial strategy in the host company is aimed at stripping labour out of production, controlling trade unions and undermining employee autonomy (Williams et al., 1992).

The lean production perspective within the 'Japanization' literature
The interest in the 'Japanization' debate has also taken the form of a focus on the effect of new manufacturing initiatives, such as JIT, on the design of jobs. These represent attempts to link the introduction of 'new or lean production' methods to competitiveness. For example, Buckley and Carter (1999: 80) claim that 'gaining value from the intangible assets a firm possesses is a key component in achieving the strongest possible competitive stance.' The diffusion of Japanese work systems is seen as a consequence of 'deliberate organizational redesign (usually by managers) to accommodate conflicting pulls from local and imported patterns, to improve the internal fit within the organization and fit with external environment and to improve the organization's performance' (Westney, 1999, p.402). This has led to debates on convergence of institutional systems that become uniform or isomorphic with the 'globalization' of managerial structures and strategies. For example, US firms in some industrial sectors have been seen as converging towards the Japanese employment system (see Lincoln and Kalleberg, 1985). The evolution in the internal organization of firms towards what is claimed to be 'welfare corporatism' is assumed to override 'market individualism' (ibid.). The changes made in business enterprises and regulatory institutions are said to be in the direction of restructuring of mass production industry by adopting new technologies and new practices (Womack et al., 1990). The focus in such arguments is on business and craft production as well as engineering, industrial relations and production restructuring – in brief, flexible manufacturing systems – to meet the Japanese challenge.

During the 1960s there was a widely held view that the diffusion of manufacturing technologies and divisions of labour at the societal level would eventually lead to convergence in institutional arrangements (see Hollingsworth and Boyer, 1997). However, despite increasing international integration of production and markets, institutional harmonization across nations has not occurred. It is commonly believed, especially among advocates of the 'lean production' perspective (such as Womack et al., 1990; MacDuffie, 1995), that there is an optimal solution for organizing labour, raw materials and capital in the manufacture and distribution of goods, and this in turn implies a set of 'best practices' for organizing work systems cross-nationally. There is an attempt to establish the optimum balance between cost reduction, retention of control and devolution of responsibility to the supply chain (for example Alford et al., 2000).

Within this perspective, the focus has been primarily on the conditions for the successful diffusion of work systems. Such systems are conceptualized as comprising modules of practices that can be disassembled, encapsulated in 'actionable consulting packages and "how to" books' (Lillrank, 1995: 976) and transplanted to another context. It is far too common to look simply for pieces of the work systems that one can benchmark and adopt. Although it is argued that 'lean production proponents argue that this system successfully combines social and technical aspects of efficient manufacturing' (Delbridge, 1998, p. 6), there is greater focus on diffusable explicit components of the system that provides a 'universal model of best practice' than on tacit components.

At the organizational level, it is argued that 'the greater the dependence of an organization on another organization, the more similar it will become to that organization in structure, climate and behavioural focus' (DiMaggio and Powell, 1991, p. 74). The advocates of the lean production perspective are less sympathetic to the notion that capitalist systems are diverse. It is assumed that work systems can be abstracted from the wider institutional context in which they are embedded (for example Womack et al., 1990).[3] According to Kenney and Florida (1993), the most successful firms use teams, quality control activities, rotation and egalitarian management styles. The 'one best solution' to organizing resources in an attempt to access technology, know-how, managerial expertise, capital and international markets (Child and Faulkner, 1998) is based on the assumption that Japanese methods are universal and can be effectively applied to other contexts. This thinking is especially reflected in the early instances of adoption, characterized by the diffusion of one or two particular management techniques, in isolation from the broader strategy and philosophy by UK management (Beale, 1994).

The 'universalistic models' in the 'Japanization' literature emphasize the 'transfer' of work systems that can be communicated between the sender (or the broadcaster) and the receiver in a form abstracted from the wider social networks. Although patterns of knowledge flow are examined across industries and countries within the universalistic accounts, the complex ensembles of routines that can mould what is being 'communicated' are ignored. Knowledge ingrained in work systems is, rather, understood as an object that can be created, packaged and diffused, more or less unchanged, from one context to another. Attention is given to immediate contingencies of a given transaction away from the scope for social action in shaping such a transaction (Scarbrough, 1995). The theoretical assumption is that key variables, such as structure and technology, move without friction and in a linear fashion (Clark, 1987). However, such variables in reality are shaped by organizational culture and value systems, and thus are sensitive to contexts. The assumption that variables move in a linear fashion implies that learning occurs in either a mimetic or a coercive way, and that 'best practice' is diffused through imitation.

The user-oriented perspective within the innovation processes literature
Research on innovation processes is also relevant for understanding the diffusion of work systems. This tends to adopt either a *supply-focused approach* (see Rogers' 1983 work on diffusion of innovations), or a *user-oriented perspective* (for example Clark et al., 1992). The supply-focused model highlights the ways in which suppliers may communicate new ideas to users in order to encourage adoption. As the focus in this model is on adoption, implementation problems tend to be ignored (Clark, 1987). It is assumed that work systems remain unmodified in their move through different sectors, units or nations. On the other hand, the user-oriented perspective considers plurality of actors, the role of social structures, unintended outcomes of power struggles and the problems with appropriating new work practices alongside existing practice and context. The user-oriented perspective thus assumes that innovations are 'heterogeneous complexes rather than homogeneous entities' (Clark, 1987, p. 60), hence their diffusion can be non-linear. This section focuses on the latter view as applied to work systems diffusion, given its closer fit with the aims of the present study.[4] Innovation in the user-oriented perspective is regarded as dependent on contextual features that are shaped by the societal context, leading to differences in implementation across contexts, including nations (see Swan et al., 1999). This view assumes that 'potential users [of the diffused knowledge or innovation] are embedded in complex ensembles of routines which may inhibit or enable their ability to use an innovation' (Clark and Newell, 1993: 70, brackets added). Hence, the limits to implementation owing to the embeddedness of diffused knowledge are addressed here. Furthermore, cognitive and political dimensions of the process of knowledge diffusion are acknowledged. It is assumed that innovations are firm-specific and socially constructed artefacts, hence they can be shaped by the interests of suppliers and powerful users. This perspective acknowledges different forms of knowledge and patterns of 'knowing as a dynamic activity involving the continuous creation, reproduction, modification and destruction of streams of meaning' (Marshall and Sapsed, 2000, p. 2). In other words, there is a stronger focus on agency. In contrast to the focus on structural and technical concerns of the supply-focused model, there is a focus on active process involving 'the formation, redesign and implementation of new ideas' in the user-oriented account (Hislop et al., 1998: 429).

The intangible questions of culture, commitment, motivation, involvement and trust are seen to be just as important as the tangibles in the diffusion of knowledge in the user-oriented perspective (Scarbrough et al., 1998). In spite of the strength of this perspective in explaining the process of work systems diffusion, there are limitations that the current study attempts to address. Some of the limitations are as follows:

1. There is limited attention to macro diffusion processes at an industry or a national level, with the exception of a handful of examples, such as Jeremy's (1981 in Clark, 1987, p. 162) work on the 'transfer of British textile technology, technique and knowledge into the USA between 1790 and 1830'.
2. The attention given to institutional characteristics, such as employment systems, organizational structures (Hedlund, 1994), and sector-specific labour markets (Lam, 2000) is scant.

An investigation of the diffusion of knowledge-driven work systems in the manufacturing sector can benefit from the arguments presented in the field of innovation-related research. It can highlight the role of the adopter or user in the internalization of 'new' work systems.

The neo-institutional literature

A multiplicity and diversity of neo-institutional arguments have had in common the questioning of conventional organizational theories. These theories rely on understanding organizations as essentially closed systems, working to a logic of efficiency, context-free rational agency and/or 'one best way' in organizational structuring and operating (Djelic, 1999). In contrast, the neo-institutional arguments put emphasis on the 'varied ways in which social groups [are] constituted inside and outside organisations and their continuous competition for control of resources' (Whitley, 1999c, p. 12). There is a belief that the rules of the competitive game are socially constituted by different state structures and policies and institutionalized patterns of behaviour, and so differ significantly between institutional contexts. Emphasis is placed on 'the shaping of recursive patterns of corporate or inter-firm behaviour by national institutions both in functionally significant areas of business such as education and training, finance etc. as well as upon underlying familial patterns of socialisation' (Loveridge and Mueller, 2000, p. 221).

The diversity of neo-institutional arguments stems from different traditions, namely from economics, sociology and political science. Differences between these arguments mean that the definition of the term 'institutions' adopted in each case also differs. Within the neo-institutional theory, there have been two broad schools of thought in comparative research – those who argue for isomorphism or convergence of social systems of production (such as DiMaggio and Powell, 1991), and those who examine contextualities in industrial organization and set out to explain the persistence or divergence of particular structural and cultural legacies across national boundaries (such as Loveridge, 1996; Streeck, 1996; Djelic, 1998). Those who examine the contextualities in industrial organization address the gap in research where there is a less developed body of work that examines the process of work systems diffusion in manufacturing settings beyond the technical and/or structural aspects of work systems as solutions to manufacturing settings' competitiveness. For instance, organizational theorists and strategists (such as Richter and Vettel, 1995; Appleyard, 1996) have acknowledged the strategic importance of the diffusion of organizational practices, but have given less importance to the institutional limits to such diffusions in terms of conflicting structural and cultural legacies and embeddedness of work systems in these legacies. 'There is evidence to suggest that these transfers are not always smooth and successful' (Kostova, 1999: 308). For example, there is much research that reports on the local adoption of 'Japanese' work systems. The resulting picture is far from a replica of a discrete set of these systems (for example Reitsperger, 1986; Elger and Smith, 1994; Mair, 1998). As was discussed earlier, proponents of the lean production perspective fail to address the limits to adoption of alternative work systems. Although the present study does not disregard the positive implications of the diffusion of work systems, such as the combination of technical skills for innovation, physical resources for economies of scale and efficiency and building of market capabilities for flexibility (see for example Aiken and Hage, 1968; Bergquist et al., 1995; Sierra, 1995; Child and Faulkner, 1998), it focuses on the limitations to diffusion as these have received limited attention.

The multiplicity of neo-institutional arguments can be broadly merged under the rational choice and historical neo-institutional typologies. The barriers to the diffusion of knowledge-driven work systems are discussed within the second typology, that is historical neo-institutionalism.

Rational choice neo-institutionalism
According to Djelic (1999), rational choice neo-institutionalism, or institutional economics, emerged as an antithesis of classical and behavioural theory in economics and political science. Within this perspective, institutions are seen as comprising 'constitutive and regulative rules or normative expectations' that are, to a degree, taken for granted or internalized by a group of actors (Abell, 1995). They are identified with the relatively rational pursuit of goals. Institutions constitute 'copying or mimetic action and

learning by adaptation' (ibid., p. 11). In other words, institutions are transmitted mimetically in groups, resonating an evolutionary epistemology.

There is a focus on the conditions facing firms in general, rather than the internal activities that contribute to the success of individual firms. Firms are seen as reactors to the environment. 'The internal decision-making process is irrelevant, and the firm is treated as if it is a single entity, a single brain' (Rowlinson, 1997, p. 14). In other words, the deterministic outlook on a firm's nature and functioning does not take into account a firm's ability to enact its environment. However, 'gigantic multinational corporations can exercise an economic stranglehold backed by the political force of the country and the local capitalistic classes' (Worsley, 1982, p. 13).

Rational choice neo-institutionalism highlights the 'plurality of governance and organizational structures [as being] reconciled with assumptions of rationality and efficiency' (Djelic, 1999, p. 5). Different industries or specific market environments are seen as bearing different structural arrangements that are most efficient in a given context. Williamson's (1985) assumptions of bounded rationality and logic of efficiency, as applied to institutionalism, drive the process of transformation in different contexts towards a particular equilibrium solution. There is an emphasis on statistics of equilibrium states rather than dynamics. In other words, there is an undersocialized conception of human action and the impact of social structure and social relations on production, distribution or consumption (see Granovetter, 1985). However, institutions can be constrained by ongoing social relations. Loveridge (1996, p. 2) contends that 'institutional evolution is seen as an ongoing process, subject to prevailing demands of the evolving needs of the actors, rather than as the end point of an apparently linear trajectory'. As Granovetter (1985: 504) argues, 'most behaviour is closely embedded in networks of interpersonal relations.' Behaviour may be aimed not only at economic goals but also at sociability, approval, status and power. Such arguments contrast with the conventional efficiency arguments within the rational choice model in economics, for rational choice neo-institutionalists do not argue for a superior, universal model. Rather, they adopt a contingency approach to transaction cost economics in association with organizational structures (or contextual rationality). Actors in this framework are defined as bounded rational with decontextualized goals. Granovetter (1985: 481) notes that 'much of the utilitarian tradition, including classical and neo-classical economics, assumes rational, self-interested behaviour affected minimally by social relations, thus invoking an idealized state.' Hence, there is limited appreciation of the role of strategic choice, beliefs and power. Behavioural characteristics such as stakeholder relations and personnel motivations are not emphasized, for the assumptions of perfect information and atomization of actors do not necessitate strategy formulation incorporating stakeholder relationships and innovative capabilities with reference to institutional constraints on choices. Although social institutions matter in the rational choice neo-institutional perspective, they are only seen as parameters in social actors' calculative decision. There is the assumption that decision-making is based on 'solipsistically acting rational individuals' (Lane and Bachmann, 1997: 231), or, in Marini's (1992, p. 21) terms, on purposive actors who 'act in ways that tend to produce beneficial results' or maximize net return.

Rational choice neo-institutionalism is characterized by its 'reconciliation of convergence with a plurality of solutions or models, each one of those being a better fitted, or more efficient type of context or environment' (Djelic, 1999, p. 4). This perspective is in alignment with the neo-contingency arguments whereby a range of factors or environmental characteristics are linked to rates of adoption and outcomes of implementing innovation processes. For example, Porter (1990) stresses the importance of nations that are 'characterized by their peculiar capabilities within particular sectors in which they have developed a regional comparative advantage' (Loveridge, 1996, p. 4). By contrast, historical neo-institutionalism (which is detailed in the following section) acknowledges goals, preferences of actors, their problem identification process and the historical contexts in which they are embedded. Managerial preferences, normative patterns and political contingencies can affect patterns of growth (Penrose, 1959). Furthermore, decision-making can be influenced by the divergent interests of individuals within and outside the organization (Brunsson, 1989). Historical neo-institutionalism rejects the very idea of convergence and argues for a multiplicity of models. Organizational solutions are defined through a historical process where both path dependencies and unanticipated developments play a part.

In the context of work systems diffusion, the rational choice neo-institutionalist arguments tend to centre on the perception that actors can copy the practices of a particular institutional environment easily to another context (see discussion on the lean production perspective within the 'Japanization' literature).

Historical neo-institutionalism
The historical neo-institutional perspective enriches the classical approach to cross-national diffusion of knowledge-driven work systems, providing a sense of the mechanisms and limits to diffusion. It allows one to discuss the barriers to diffusion, a matter rarely treated in the literature. In contrast to conventional efficiency accounts, 'historical variants of neo-institutionalism have generally set out to account for the peculiarities of a given national system of industrial production and for persistent

structural differences across national boundaries' (Djelic, 1999, p. 7).[5]
Historical neo-institutionalism reflects the 'societal effects' (Sorge, 1991)
approach to work systems diffusion, in that nationally embedded
differences across business systems are acknowledged in the process of
diffusing alternative work systems. Within this perspective, national structural and cultural legacies are traced as a means of determining what
makes a national system.

Although advocates of this perspective broadly agree that economic
activity is embedded within a particular set of national institutional constraints, they differ in their focus on the constraining legacies. Some
researchers (such as Tolbert and Zucker, 1983; March and Olsen, 1984;
Hamilton and Biggart, 1988; Fligstein, 1990) place emphasis on the structural aspects of institutions, investigating mainly the regulative carriers of
institutions. Others have adopted a more sociological or cultural view,
focusing on cognitive and normative carriers of institutions, that is values,
expectations and belief systems (for example Whitley, 1992). In such a view,
cultural mechanisms are taken to increase stability of the work environment
and to facilitate the equitable mediation of transactions between parties
under conditions that severely limit the capacity for rational control.[6]

Historical neo-institutionalism acknowledges the peculiarities of each
national institutional context. Hence it rejects the assumption that institutional contexts are homogeneous. Social relationships and the impact that
collective norms have on these relationships are examined in conjunction
with the historical underpinnings and structural embeddedness of the
given ties (Djelic, 1999). Institutional change and deinstitutionalization are
influenced by social pressures associated with the diversity in beliefs, practices and social expectations that can hinder the continuation of a practice
(see Dacin et al., 2002). As opposed to a static framework provided by
rational choice neo-institutionalism in the analysis of the effects of cooperation, historical neo-institutionalism offers a more articulated view of the
characteristics of technology, role of knowledge, nature of the firm and
dynamics of competition, considering the cognitive dimension of the innovation process (see Colombo, 1998). For instance, although market opportunities lead to innovations in organizational design, these innovations are
not necessarily the outcomes of rational lines of thinking about the most
efficient way to organize. Organizational practices, rather, represent legitimated structures and cultural understandings (Hamilton and Biggart,
1988). The sensitivity to the historical context of work systems or to path-
dependencies does not allow for 'best practices' of a particular institutional
environment to be uniformly imitated by the adopters embedded in a
different institutional setting. For example, Patel and Pavitt's (1997) study
of 400 of the world's largest firms shows that their technological compe-

tencies are influenced by the firms' principal products and the conditions in their home country. It is claimed that managers are heavily constrained in the directions of their technological search given the 'complexity and path dependency in the accumulation of firm-specific technological competencies' (ibid.: 141). Historical neo-institutionalism is sensitive to national contexts, or what Clark (2000) calls the 'zones of manoeuvre' (which will be defined in Section Three of this chapter). In other words, path dependencies, or pre-existing capabilities inherent in contexts and firms, can enable or limit strategic choice intended to contribute to a firm's performance.

The basic premise of historical neo-institutionalism is that specific organizational and behavioural tendencies are shaped by certain features of a given institutional setting that is constructed in an evolutionary manner (see for example Nelson and Winter, 1982). This yields what Boyer (1997) calls 'capitalist diversity'. In other words, the institutionalization of market relations is the result of synchronization and legitimization of reactions to crises that have developed in a previous system, and reflect 'the social and political conflict particular to each country'. The institutional framework of a nation is taken as an ideal form, specific to a social pattern, based on the following argument:

> Where key institutions structuring the nature of property rights and their enforcement, of economic actors, and of the norms governing their interaction are more strongly established at the regional or supranational levels, then we would expect distinctive patterns of economic organization to become more established within those boundaries. (Whitley, 1999a: 118)

For example, Britain and the US tend to be characterized by market-oriented capitalism, and founded on the institutional characteristics of decentralization, external mobility, role of the market and low level of mediation with trade unions. On the other hand, Japan is seen as characterized by high market regulation, institutional cooperation, a credit-based financial system and paternalist authority relations. (Further discussion can be found in the following subsection on 'divergent capitalisms'.) The institutional characteristics of Britain and the US provide for 'rapid response to recession' and 'adjustment to structural changes' (Boyer, 1997, p. 90). Similarly, Whitley (1999c) has documented the character of divergent capitalist systems, or in his words multiple 'national business systems' (NBSs), as distinct. The multiplicity of cultural and structural legacies suggests the co-existence of national patterns of organizing rather than their reconciliation. This derives from the assumption of historical neo-institutionalism that each national institutional background is unique and persistent, explaining significant differences in organizational structuring and operating across national boundaries (Djelic, 1999). Consequently, the diffusion of work systems from one institutional context to another can be constrained by 'persistent differences' in patterns of organizing. In simple terms, 'choices [have] been made long ago and [are] deeply entrenched in an established "culture" that [is] at least in the short term, beyond the reach of contemporary actors' (Crouch and Streeck, 1997, p. 1). In contrast to the environmentally deterministic nature of change within rational choice neo-institutionalism, it is the change in institutional features that initiates organizational change within historical neo-institutionalism. Organizational change – the internalization of new work systems in the study reported here – is seen as more than a process of adaptation driven by rational actors along lines of efficiency. There is, rather, editing of knowledge-driven work systems, given the constraints and path dependencies on diffusion. Historical neo-institutionalism highlights the stickiness of pre-existing institutional legacies, generally defined at the national level and with an impact on actions at the organizational level.

This book adopts the historical neo-institutionalist, as opposed to the rational choice neo-institutionalist, perspective in an attempt to address the limits to diffusion of context-dependent knowledge-driven work systems. The focus is on examining the interplay between the context and process of diffusion. (Further justification for the adoption of this perspective can be found in the section on 'comparing perspectives within Japanization, innovation processes and neo-institutional literatures'.) The book draws a distinction between institutional characteristics at the macro national level (such as the financial system, state, legal system, public training system and union strength) and those at the meso local level (such as the location of the company, skills base in the region, and level of industrial dispute, discussed in Section Three of this chapter). Given this analytic line of demarcation, the perspective adopted in this book differs from others that do not separate the national institutional characteristics from the local institutional characteristics (such as Karnøe, 1995; Erramilli, 1996). It should also be emphasized that there is a focus here on dominant institutional characteristics that govern resources, such as labour and finances. In practice, few countries are expected to have developed all the institutional characteristics 'for any single coherent way of organizing economic activities to be institutionalized as the dominant one' (Whitley, 2000b: 858).

The differences in the institutional and societal infrastructures and networking arrangements can lead to variations in internalization of work systems (see Swan et al., 1999). This suggests a neo-institutional rather than a neo-contingency interpretation. The aim here is not to highlight the need to achieve compatibility between work systems and the task environment, or to identify systems that are seen as the most efficient at particular points in time, as do scholars such as Miles and Snow (1978). Rather, there is an attempt to consider the contextual influences and the role of actors in work systems diffusion involving the interaction of technology, organization and society (Slappendel, 1996). It should be noted that the historical neo-institutional approach adopted here cannot be subsumed under the neo-contingency framework, but a basic contingency argument is inevitable. As Sorge (1991: 186) argues, 'whenever a correspondence between markets, strategies, organization and human resources is postulated or recognized, the argument which makes this explicit is potentially or even necessarily a neo-contingency one'. It is desirable to have a fit between institutional regimes and the diffusion process to extend the explanatory power of the analytic framework used in this study. Loveridge (1998: 1049) contends that 'much of the characterization of national systems in the institutionalist literature has been based on the broadest of generalizations that sometimes appear to have gained credibility through repeated mutual citation'. There is an attempt in this book to fine-tune such generalizations through an empirical evidence of actors' influence at the organizational level on the diffusion process.

Divergent capitalisms
Various studies conducted within neo-institutionalism argue for the variation in actors' ability to act legitimately across institutional settings, for example, the following: Maurice et al. (1986) and Sorge (1991) on the 'societal effects' on work systems; Whitley (1992–2000) on 'national business systems'; Dobbin (1995) on the embeddedness of economic rationality in institutional norms and conventions; Hollingsworth and Boyer (1997) on 'social systems of production'; Herrigal (1996) on 'industrial orders' in Germany and the US; and Hamilton and Biggart (1988), Orrù et al. (1991) on post-war East Asian capitalisms. Each institutional context is believed to have developed 'in contrasting ways as a result of pre-industrial legacies, patterns of industrialization and twentieth-century state structures and policies' (Whitley, 1999b, p.16). Among the historical neo-institutional arguments listed, those on divergent capitalisms are the most appropriate in explaining the different forms of economic organization in different national contexts. Given that our aim is to provide a detailed, systematic and rigorous comparison of the extent to which work systems are internalized in a 'foreign' institutional environment, a framework that is sensitive to contextualities and pays systematic attention to the influence of social institutions is essential in providing answers to the central research question.

The research focuses on Whitley's (1992–2000) work on divergent capitalisms. This work is concerned with 'describing and explaining variations in economic organization regardless of whether they become established in geographical regions, states or continents' (Whitley, 1999a: 117). It addresses the development of each institutional context in contrasting ways as a result of pre-industrial legacies. The central motive of the divergent capitalisms view is to account for the existence and persistence of nationally distinct forms of economic organization. Although this view encompasses research into the social constitution of the underlying processes, it does not adopt a processual perspective to cross-national comparisons. The key element in the framework is the firm, which is conceptualized as the dominant unit of governance, differing across national systems. Examples include the 'chaebol' in South Korea and the 'keiretsu' in Japan. The divergent capitalisms view highlights key macro-level institutions that are seen as shaping different forms of business systems. Whitley (1996, 2000a) identifies the governance principles of each market economy or business system as the state, financial system, public training system, legal system, authority relations and union strength. The degree of standardization of coordination and forms of economic organization are commonly observed in these principles or systems. The key institutional features combine to form six types of business systems: fragmented, coordinated industrial district, compartmentalized, state organized, collaborative and highly coordinated (see Table 1.1). Each of these systems is seen as reflecting the principles of domination of their institutional environments (Whitley, 1999b).

Variations in institutional features arise from the fact that institutionalized rules are enacted in a non-uniform way. Given the embeddedness of organizations in larger social relations (Granovetter, 1985), principles of governance would be expected to differ across business systems. In other words, the way in which managerial coordination and work organization of the firm are brought together reflects the institutional context in which the organization is embedded. When organizations extend their operations into new institutional contexts, they are highly likely to adapt their existing structures and cultures. Institutional constraints can affect the degree to which work systems are diffused to the host country (Morgan et al., 2000b).

The work on divergent capitalisms has been extended to include organizational characteristics. As will be discussed in Chapter Two, these include, among others, task fragmentation, worker discretion and involvement, managerial control of work organization, separation of managers from workers and employer commitment to employment security (Whitley, 1999b).

This research focuses on the structural and cultural legacies of two of the six business environments: 'highly coordinated' and 'compartmentalized' systems, as the empirical investigation is undertaken in Anglo-Japanese settings alone. Japan exemplifies the 'highly coordinated' business system, whereas the US/UK context typifies the 'compartmentalized' system (Whitley, 1999b). It is recognized here that there is a wide variation among firms within Japan. Nonetheless, as a whole, Japanese MNCs tend to

Table 1.1   The institutional characteristics of different business systems

Type of business system/Key features*	Fragmented	Coordinated industrial district	Compartmentalized	State organized	Collaborative	Highly coordinated
State	Predatory	Considerably coordinating locally but limited nationally	Regulative	Coordinating and developing	Considerably coordinating	Coordinating and developing
Financial system	Low risk-sharing by banks	Some local bank risk-sharing	Capital market-based	Credit-based	Credit-based	Credit-based
Public training system	Weak	Strong	Limited in scope and effectiveness	Limited	Broad in scope and strong	Limited
Legal system	Weak	Considerably reliable	Reliable	Considerably weak	Reliable	Considerably reliable
Authority relations	Paternalistic	Limited communitarian	Contractual	Highly paternalist	Highly communitarian	Highly paternalist
Union strength	Low	High	Low	Limited	High	Limited

Note: The effect of key features in each business environment is observed under ceteris paribus conditions.

Source: Adapted from Whitley (1999b, p. 60 and 2000a).

exhibit commonality in their Japan-based systems with regard to work organization, labour relations and employee development. Hence the underlying philosophies, such as team-based work, ambiguous job descriptions, a seniority-based reward system, staffing from within and training through job rotation, remain the same.

Highly coordinated business systems   According to Sako (1997), the organizational integration of economic activities is associated with the national system of industrial relations. High levels of integration are observed in environments characterized by high levels of state risk-sharing, strong intermediaries and high market regulations, coupled with some union strength, limited public training system and high trust in formal institutions (Whitley, 1999b). Such environments encourage collaboration between actors, and develop highly coordinated systems where risks can easily be shared and the state plays a highly coordinating role.[7] For example, studies in Japanese business systems (such as Orrù, 1997) show that institutional cooperation is a key feature of the overarching organizational logic of highly coordinated business systems. In the context of cross-national diffusion of work systems, firms operating in highly coordinated business systems are not likely to be involved in diffusing central activities that are closely linked to domestic partners and agencies. 'They [highly coordinating systems] find it difficult to shift key activities and significant resources to foreign locations, and moreover are unlikely to see the need for such investment as long as their domestic location and commitments are viewed as providing major advantages' (Whitley, 1999c, p. 12). Given their strong embeddedness in a network of mutual obligations and commitment (Gerlach, 1992; Sako, 1992; McMillan, 1996), firms in these systems tend to implement incremental, continuous and interdependent change. This means such firms are more likely to constrain their radical diversification into related fields. A credit-based financial system also has a role to play in this, as banks (which tend to have strong links with their clients) become reluctant to invest in unrelated industries. Hence, there is less of an opportunity for an entrepreneurial function. However, this does not imply that firms in highly coordinated systems have limited firm-specific competences. As is suggested by Whitley (2000b: 878, brackets added), 'skills are more firm dependent and specific [in highly coordinated business systems such as Japan] than in economies with strong public training systems organized around existing industries [as that in Germany].' As will be shown in Chapter Two, there is greater emphasis on tacit work systems and, hence, greater work-system specificity in highly coordinated NBSs. There is a lock-in to growth goals with credit-based financial system and long-term employer-employee relations. Such relations based on mutual obligations limit opportunistic behaviour and allow for considerable trust between actors, as well as major knowledge and risk-sharing. This institutional characteristic may not prevail in other business systems, and its absence may facilitate the diffusion of work systems to other contexts. However, the strong connection also means that actors may find it difficult to exit the network when prevailing conditions change (see for example Zysman, 1983). Furthermore, the institutional arrangements of highly coordinated systems, such as reciprocal paternalist authority relations, encourage investment in skills development. These skills are typically firm-specific due to long-term commitments and an 'experience' model of education (Hibino, 1997), encompassing in-house training and job rotation (Dore and Sako, 1997).

The 'structure and flow' aspects (Sorge, 1996, p. 73) of highly coordinated institutions form distinct national patterns, in which firms and inter-firm relations are governed within a tightly knit network. Sorge (1996) conceptualizes the structural aspects as the properties that characterize the composition of a group of people or of a system, such as different types of labour based on age, experience, specialism and learning. The flow aspects refer to 'additions and subtractions which occur with regard to a dimension over a certain period of time', such as labour market mobility between firms (ibid., p. 73).

Embeddedness in a tightly knit network can have negative implications for the diffusability of work systems from strongly institutionalized environments that limit opportunistic behaviour and depend on considerable trust between social partners to contexts exhibiting low extent of alliance integration (Whitley, 2000a). In other words, highly localized, context-dependent work systems can be 'sticky' to diffuse to other institutional contexts. Allied hierarchies, commonly observed in highly coordinated business systems, tend to allow for limited diffusability of firm-specific competitive advantages to foreign subsidiaries and limited subsidiary development of distinct organizational capabilities, given their highly embedded nature (Whitley, 1999b). Such hierarchies are seen as internationalizing more slowly and incrementally than firms in, for example, compartmentalized business systems. 'A more common pattern of internationalization for firms in highly co-ordinated environments is to rely initially on exports because of their dependence on business partners and employees for competitive advantage' (ibid., p. 21). Societal patterns may not be reproduced in different contexts even where an oncoming innovation is basically similar, for 'changes are not the same in every society, even when we are dealing with technical challenges' (Sorge, 1996, p. 81).

The discussion of the institutional characteristics of highly coordinated business systems allows one to claim that the knowledge-driven work systems of firms in highly coordinated business systems are likely to be less

diffusable to other institutional environments. The variation in labour
market institutions, state structures and policies and financial systems in
different societies can discourage the diffusability of knowledge-driven
work systems to other firms. (This will be further explained in Chapter Two.)

Compartmentalized business systems   The compartmentalized business
system, in which UK organizational practices are embedded, differs greatly
from the highly coordinated system in its institutionalized procedures regu-
lating business practice and the norms governing market boundaries. In less
integrated or embedded contexts of economic relations with relatively easy
market entry and exit, such as those of the US and the UK, the dominant
institutions discourage cooperation and collaboration between business
partners, including employers and employees. Work systems or organizational practices of firms in compartmentalized business systems are not
strongly embedded in social networks of close cooperation and high interdependency. This is illustrated by the member firms' low capacity for collective problem-solving (compare Lane and Bachmann, 1997). Relations
between actors are defined as 'arm's length' and typically adversarial.[8]
Firms are relatively isolated from each other. Consequently, the influence of
employee interests and business partners on decision-making is low, as is frequently reported in studies of Japanese operations in the UK (such as
Murata and Harrison, 1991). This has negative implications for continuous
innovation and the development of long-term growth strategies. There is,
rather, a reliance on a strongly institutionalized formal system of rules and
procedures that facilitates delegation and trust in formal institutions. Trust
is governed 'contractually' rather than through 'obligational contracting'
(Sako, 1992). For example, Kester (1996, p. 108) suggests Anglo-American
corporate governance emphasizes 'the reduction of agency costs associated
with the separation of ownership from control, relying more heavily on
formal, legalistic mechanisms to order commercial relationships among
transacting parties'. The coordinating role of the state is limited. The state
acts more as a regulator, where 'finance flows through competitive capital
markets rather than banks, and training is more a matter for individual
investment than for coordinated collaboration between state agencies,
employers and unions', creating a predictable environment in which rationality of decision-making can be highlighted to a greater extent (Whitley,
1999c, p. 8). This has the implication that organizational practices of compartmentalized business systems are more diffusable to other institutional
environments. The limited collaboration, short-termism, weak control
systems and fragmented training systems in compartmentalized institutional environments tend to generate work systems that are easier to diffuse
than those of highly coordinated environments.

Individualism and limited conventions governing roles in compartmentalized business systems (see for example Lewchuk's (1992) discussion of the diffusion of Fordist technology in Britain) may foster entrepreneurialism in firms. However, this may not necessarily reflect firms' capability to develop a firm-specific or idiosyncratic knowledge base. As Lane (1996, p. 276, brackets added) argues, 'lack of support for favourable access to capital, skill and R&D [in compartmentalized business systems] . . . has reinforced the risk-aversion and short-termism fostered by the [capital market-based] financial system', which can discourage the development of a firm-specific knowledge base.

Compartmentalized business systems are also linked to fragmented training systems. In other words, skills training and control systems are identified as weak. Limited collaboration between employers, unions and other groups tends to discourage cooperation in the management of training systems (Whitley, 1999b). It is argued that 'while collaboration between functions has improved, the level of dismantlement of these internal vertical specializations is only slowly taking effect in Western firms' (Mueller and Loveridge, 1997, p. 146). As commitment and mutual dependence are limited, employee contribution to knowledge creation is constrained. Adaptation to environmental changes is through organizational structuring rather than in-house learning and employee adaptability. The implications of these institutional features for diffusability of work systems need to be considered. Isolated hierarchies, commonly observed in these systems, do not offer the same advantages in terms of sharing idiosyncratic knowledge with employees and business partners as allied hierarchies in highly coordinated systems. Competencies are not 'constrained' by obligational ties to partners. Hence they are more mobile across borders. This deems work practices in compartmentalized business systems more diffusable to other institutional environments (Whitley, 1999b). In order to manage risk and uncertainty, firms in compartmentalized systems are more likely to move assets across sectors and gain experience of managing diverse activities. They are also more likely to delegate autonomy to subsidiaries, and encourage the adoption of polycentric rather than ethnocentric strategies.[9] As Whitley (1999c, p. 20) contends, firms in compartmentalized business systems 'are likely to assume that their firm specific competitive advantages can be equally successful abroad as at home . . . since [organizational competences are] not closely tied to particular links with local business partners and institutions'.

Comparing perspectives within Japanization, innovation processes and neo-institutional literatures
As is shown in Table 1.2, the four major perspectives as applied to knowledge-driven work systems diffusion differ from each other in some important

Table 1.2 Comparison of four major perspectives

Approach	Key authors	Major focus	Dominant level of investigation	Framework used	View of work systems diffusion
The labour process perspective within the Japanization literature	Briggs (1988); Dickens and Savage (1988); Delbridge (1998)	Comparison of work processes *within* firms in different countries	Intra-firm	Universalistic understanding of the control-related nature of Japanese work systems	Not considered
The lean production perspective within the Japanization literature	Womack et al. (1990); Kenney and Florida (1993); MacDuffie (1995)	Comparison of work structures and technicalities *between* firms in different countries	Inter-firm	Universalistic view of work systems as best practices	Objectified
The user-oriented perspective within the innovation processes literature	Swan and Clark (1992); Scarbrough et al. (1998); Scarbrough and Swan (1999); Marshall and Sapsed (2000)	Comparison of innovation development *within* firms and across projects	Intra-firm	Acknowledges embeddedness of work systems	Context-dependent
The historical neo-institutional perspective within the neo-institutional literature	Sorge (1991); Hollingsworth and Boyer (1997); Djelic (1999); Whitley (1992–2000)	Systematic comparison of nationally distinct patterns of organization, including structures and processes in different countries	Inter-firm	Acknowledges embeddedness of work systems in broader institutional arrangements	Context-dependent

aspects. It should be noted that the distinction drawn in this table is not based on a comprehensive list of mutually exclusive features of the four major perspectives. The table is a schematic presentation of the dominant characteristics of each perspective in comparison to the others. Marked differences in the table concern the focus (processes versus technical and/or structural properties of firms), the level of investigation (intra-firm versus inter-firm), the nature of the framework (universal versus embedded) and the view of work systems diffusion (objectified versus context-dependent or sedimented). The attention paid to the nature and historical roots of social institutions also differs among the different perspectives.

With reference to the research aim, it is essential to select a perspective that provides a systematic and rigorous comparison of the levels of implementation and internalization of Japanese work systems in 'foreign' institutional environments. The labour process view within the Japanization literature presents a universalistic approach to the control-related aim of introducing Japanese work practices. Although this view focuses more on processes than technical and structural properties of firms (which is in line with the aim of the current research), it predominantly investigates intra-firm characteristics, such as the impact of Japanese work systems on employee empowerment, rather than inter-firm organization of resources. The nature of work systems diffusion (whether it is objectified or context-dependent) is not of concern in this view. There is a focus on governance and control mechanisms implicit in the diffusion of work systems. The impact of path dependencies and institutional constraints on the internalization of such systems is not acknowledged. The universalistic understanding of the control-related nature of work systems in the labour process view within the Japanization literature is not in accordance with the purpose of the research reported here.

Nor is the 'lean production' perspective considered as suitable for forming the basis of the analytic framework. Although the level of investigation of work systems diffusion is inter-firm, this perspective ignores the contextualities in the diffusion process. It focuses on the objectified nature of work systems diffusion with an emphasis on the diffusion of work structures and technicalities. There is a universalistic view of work systems as best practices that can be diffused with ease to other contexts. Constraints on the diffusion process are not considered.

At first glance, the user-oriented perspective within the innovation processes literature seems well suited as a basis for the analytic framework in this study. This perspective focuses on processes and acknowledges the social embeddedness of work systems and the context-dependent nature of work systems diffusion. It bears similarities to the historical neo-institutional perspective with regard to the sensitivity it shows to contextual features that can lead to differences in the internalization of alternative work systems. However, studies of innovation processes adopting the user-oriented perspective have only recently aimed at investigating inter-organizational arrangements across countries (for example Swan et al., 1999). The majority of the studies adopting this perspective do not link inter-firm level investigations to the influence of institutional characteristics at a national level (Clark (1987) is an exception to this). If a link is made, this is not performed in a systematic manner. The diffusion of organizational practices themselves is not considered as a key learning activity. Rather, internal processes and strategic decisions about innovation design of user organizations are analysed.

In contrast to the user-oriented perspective within the innovation processes literature, the historical neo-institutional perspective offers a framework that links characteristics of work systems to path dependencies within particular institutional settings in a systematic manner (for example Djelic, 1998). A systematic comparison of the context-dependent nature of work systems diffusion provides a rigorous analysis of the diffusion process. The focus is not on the process of technology development but on that of diffusing organizational structures and processes, including HRM activities. The impact of key characteristics of distinct social institutions on the firm is acknowledged. This historical neo-institutional approach is different from Porter's (1990) work on the competitive advantage of nations. It is more specific, restricted to fewer countries, related to the organization and human resources literature in greater detail and informed by systematic comparisons of cases. Regarding these merits, the historical neo-institutional perspective is considered as the appropriate basis for constructing the analytic framework in this study. As the analyses using the historical neo-institutional perspective generally reside at the macro national level (see for example Herrigal, 1996), arguments are drawn from the user-oriented perspective in the innovation processes literature to formulate propositions on the diffusion process at the micro organizational level.

In the following section, a number of shortcomings are listed with regard to observations in the literature on the historical neo-institutional perspective. The limitations of the perspective are addressed in order to develop a more process-sensitive framework that can guide and structure the present study. In other words, Whitley's work on divergent capitalisms, which tends to address structure rather than agency, is furthered by linking structures to micro-level social action in which they are implicated. 'Contexts of meaning within which individuals define themselves, interpret their roles and act accordingly' are acknowledged without losing sight of the structural aspects (Karnøe and Nygaard, 1999: 85).

3. THE HISTORICAL NEO-INSTITUTIONAL PERSPECTIVE: CRITIQUE AND REFINEMENTS

The historical neo-institutional perspective adopted here provides an evolutionary, path-dependent view of transformation. It delineates more a linear, sequential process of change than a cyclical one. It does not account for instances of radical change (Djelic, 1999), and runs the risk of overlooking the possibility that organizations can be sufficiently powerful to enact their environments. In contrast to the evolutionary theory (Nelson and Winter, 1982), the historical neo-institutional perspective is concerned with the peculiarities of each institutional context that explain persistent differences in organizational structuring and operating. Although the process of change is seen as highly situation-specific and decisions are perceived as being influenced by various environmental factors, organizational solutions within historical neo-institutionalism are regarded as being defined within specific historical contexts via unanticipated developments. This draws the criticism that the historical neo-institutional perspective is static in nature. Although the historical variant of neo-institutional theory rejects the idea of convergence in organizational structuring and operating, it represents a new constraint, in that institutional contexts are seen as narrowing firms' choices with respect to strategies and solutions and as shaping goals and preferences (Hollingsworth and Boyer, 1997). The emphasis on regularity and stability (or incremental change) within this perspective rarely builds in the role of the collective or individual actor. Rather, actions are seen as predetermined by institutional conditions. However, a firm's knowledge can be 'continually re(constituted) through the activities undertaken within a firm' (Tsoukas, 1996: 22). 'Whitley offers no amplification on how [institutional] forces interact with the actors' social responses, seen to have become institutionalized within the structures he delineates' (Loveridge, 1996, p. 5, brackets added). Hence, it is proposed in the present study that the role of actors in shaping work systems is important. Attention is paid not only to structural and cultural developments in the past to arrive at explanations about present diffusion processes, but also to the role of management and the interpretation of alternative work systems by employees. The crucial factor in the internalization of such systems is the interaction between the context and the process of diffusion. There is an interest here in investigating this interplay. The historical neo-institutional perspective is refined in this study to incorporate the process dimension of the diffusion of work systems. Empirical evidence is provided to integrate actors into action and to combine action with constraints by highlighting the limitations to the diffusion process. As suggested by the arguments in the innovation processes literature (for example Hislop et al., 1998), the internalization of work systems is an active process involving actors' decisions to adopt new ideas, where the links between implementation and internalization processes are important in determining the outcome of the diffused system. Furthermore, implementation is a necessary condition for internalization of a work system, for a work system cannot be infused with value unless it is used in the organization (Kostova, 1999). Hence, context-dependent knowledge is liable to actors' interpretation upon its diffusion to a new setting. In other words, its 'utilization or development during the innovation process requires the active involvement of those workers who possess it' (Hislop et al., 1998: 438). Actors have the potential to creatively interpret their past experiences. 'Acquisition of knowledge is not a simple matter of taking in knowledge; rather things assumed to be natural categories, such as "bodies of knowledge", "learners", and "cultural transmission" require reconceptualization as cultural, social products' (Lave, 1993, p. 8). In other words, knowledge undergoes construction and transformation when put to use (Blackler, 1995).

There is a dynamic interaction among episodes of external acquisition of knowledge, its use by firms and the commitment by firms to the extent that the acquired knowledge assumes a taken-for-granted or institutionalized nature. Knowledge-driven work systems are institutionalized when 'the employees at the recipient unit attach to the practice a symbolic meaning and value, as have the employees from the home country' (Kostova, 1999: 311). Actors are a vital component of work systems that are diffused by translations to their international affiliates.

The refinement suggested here is displayed in Figure 1.1. This figure constitutes one of the building blocks of the analytic framework. It indicates that, triggered by operational and/or strategic motivations, work systems are acquired and put to use by management. The role of management is observed in the implementation of work systems. Furthermore, the acceptance of alternative work systems within the firm points to the translation of existing work systems by employees that results in appropriated work systems or the blending of 'new' work systems with the existing ones. Translation is understood as 'transformation, modification, change, renovation, and identity construction – a blending of the foreign and the local, the new and the old' (Tsui-Auch, 2001, p. 719). The adopter view of diffusion is addressed here with an emphasis on the investigation of the degree of internalization of knowledge-driven work systems. The implementation and internalization processes are viewed as ongoing processes.

It is expected that higher levels of implementation of a particular work system will be associated with higher levels of internalization of that work system. The concept of appropriation itself reflects this cumulative and progressive transformation of work systems. Where the alternative work

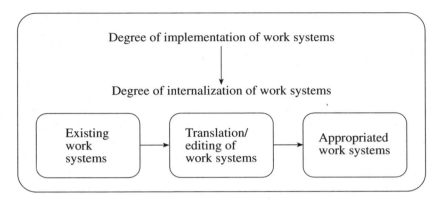

Figure 1.1 The implementation and internalization of knowledge-driven work systems

system is incompatible with the existing practices, one would expect problems in internalization (Swan and Clark, 1992). It is also possible that although a work system is formally implemented, employees may not infuse it with value by developing positive attitudes towards it. On the whole, a focus on the degree of internalization of work systems can provide important insights into the problems of diffusing alternative work systems.

The process of editing work systems is not driven by pre-existing legacies alone. Actors may not be fully constrained or determined in their values and interests. For example, they can amplify their decisions through memberships in networks. Clark (2000) contends that contexts imply 'zones of manoeuvre'. In other words, firms do not act alone nor do they 'reconfigure [their] repertoire of capabilities as a design rule except within certain degrees of freedom' (ibid., p. 304). There is co-evolution, in the sense that contexts contain constraints as well as enablers and, hence, pre-existing processes in a transitional period may lead to a new configuration. This is illustrated by Blundel and Clark's (2001) study of two cheesemakers, categorized as artisanal or craft-based firms, in the UK. Their tale of the cheesemakers shows that networks in which the firms are embedded are dynamic, idiosyncratic and living phenomena. They argue that 'inherited' factors within the specific social structures of the two cheesemakers shape learning and, hence, the growth trajectory of firms.

The level of analysis in neo-institutional research is commonly at the macro level. 'There is a pronounced need for cross-cultural scholars to conduct more micro-level research that documents what happens when managers from different cultures work together' (Brannen and Salk, 1999, p. 334). There is only a mention, rather than a detailed empirical study of the impact, of the national level on that of the organization. The national level is generally considered as the appropriate level of analysis for social institutions (Whitley, 1992). However, social patterns shaping the diffusion process at the organizational level also need to be considered. The key characteristics of the institutional environment in which a firm operates are insufficient for a detailed analysis of the implementation and internalization of work systems at the organizational level. Once again, an attempt is made to refine the historical neo-institutional perspective by complementing the national level with the organizational level. Although Whitley (1999c) defines key work systems characteristics at the organizational level in his later work, it is not clear how these systems are affected in a context of cross-national diffusion across conflicting national business systems.

The historical neo-institutional perspective also has the shortcoming of disregarding local institutional characteristics in its analysis. Mueller and Loveridge (1997, p.154) propose that 'what is perhaps required is that the interaction between the MNC and the key institutions isolated by NBS/NIS theorists should be studied in greater depth in its local context and across a range of sectors as well as a number of levels of corporate activity.'

Key contextual characteristics can be both industry-specific and site-specific. The historical neo-institutional perspective examines dominant patterns of institutional arrangement, and hence is not sensitive to different levels of implementation and internalization of work systems across different localities, such as different location sites. As is discussed in the next section, it is useful here to analyse the nature of local, in addition to national, contexts of firms. The present study addresses these shortcomings by aiming to investigate the interaction between the context and the process.

Institutional and Organizational Influences on Diffusion

The following three subsections detail the nature of the influence of national institutional, local institutional and organizational characteristics on the diffusion of work systems. Each of these sections constitutes the building blocks of the analytic framework.

Key institutional characteristics

National institutional level
Governance structures and capabilities developed in home countries can affect the nature of the investments made, where and when they are made, and how they are managed in internationalization efforts. It is suggested

that weakly institutionalized contexts of economic activity will be less conducive to developing stable and wide ranging partnerships and long-term commitments across boundaries (Whitley, 1999c). For example, particularistic environments, such as China, are notable for their weak state combined with weak norms of governing economic transactions. In contrast to weakly institutionalized settings, highly coordinated business systems, such as Japan, present strongly institutionalized systems of normative rules that lock key actors into long-term commitments, and encourage cooperative behaviour by restricting exit from business networks. Hence, highly coordinated business systems would be expected to be favourable to the internalization of work systems.[10] However, the ability of firms in such systems to diffuse their work systems to other institutional contexts is questionable. Firms in these systems are likely to 'limit the size and centrality of their initial FDI [foreign direct investment]' (Whitley, 1999c, p. 13). (This was discussed in detail in the section on 'highly coordinated business systems'.) Given the embeddedness of practices in home economies, commitments to new partnerships are expected, in general, to be limited. There is likely to be an integration of foreign subsidiaries into the parent company's operations, and linkages developing incrementally. Nevertheless, it is likely that firms in highly coordinated systems will allow their subsidiaries to learn and adopt new ways of doing things, as long as there is control over key or strategic resources.[11]

Firms operating in highly coordinated systems are very likely to adopt complex and risky innovation strategies that require a considerable amount of both tacit and explicit knowledge to develop and implement such innovations. This in turn can enhance and develop organizational capabilities (Whitley, 2000b). Skills in these institutions are 'more firm-dependent and specific than in economies with strong public training systems organized around existing industries' (ibid.: 878). Work systems are developed in-house and regarded as highly tacit and difficult to access by outsiders.

On the other hand, given the weak public training systems, the role of the state as a regulator, the flow of finance through capital markets and reliance on formalized rules and procedures (see the section on 'divergent capitalisms' for a detailed discussion), compartmentalized business systems, such as the UK, constitute a weakly institutionalized environment. Such business systems are likely to be unfavourable to the internalization of work systems, for firms in these systems are characterized by 'arm's length' relationships, and entry and exit arrangements for actors are more flexible. Firms are not constrained by obligational ties to stakeholders, including employees. Their competitive advantages are not dependent on other actors in a business network, and they are more willing to invest major resources abroad (Whitley, 1999c). As business partners cannot be relied upon to

Table 1.3   The impact of national institutional characteristics on work systems diffusion

Characteristics of work systems	Highly coordinated	Compartmentalized
Willingness to diffuse	Limited	Considerable
Diffusability of firm-specific competitive advantages to foreign subsidiaries	Limited	High
Central control of subsidiaries and integration with parent companies	Considerable	Variable
Subsidiary development of distinct organizational capabilities	Limited	Considerable
Extent to which competitive competences are firm-specific (with reference to tacitness of work systems)	High	Low

Source: Adapted from Whitley (1999c)

manage risks, firms in compartmentalized systems 'control more widely varied and unconnected activities and resources than co-operative ones' (ibid., p. 14). Consequently, they gain a broader range of experience in managing the activities of different kinds of industries. Transplants of such firms are more likely to be delegated autonomy by the parent company in developing strategies to adapt to the local context. Knowledge of such firms tends to be highly mobile given their inclination to standardize work procedures. Hence, they are likely to assume that their organizational capabilities can produce successful results abroad just as at home.

Firms operating in compartmentalized systems are highly likely to adopt innovation strategies that are often dependent on new, codified knowledge as a key to organizational competence (Whitley, 2000b). Their formalized systems are likely to be easier to diffuse than tacit knowledge. Low skills and limited employee involvement in such business systems can hinder the learning necessary to adapt to changing environmental conditions. Moreover, organizational flexibility is likely to be inhibited by the standardization of knowledge and limited accumulation of tacit knowledge (Lazonick, 1998).

The results of the above discussion are summarized in Table 1.3.

Local institutional level

In addition to the impact of institutional variation at the national level, local institutional characteristics can have an effect on the implementation and internalization of Japanese knowledge-driven work systems. The salient characteristics that are considered in the present research are the company location area and site, the skills base and the level of industrial dispute in a given region.

A number of research studies carried out in the area of 'Japanization' have examined the impact of local labour supply and industrial relations of transplants on work organization (for example Elger and Smith, 1994; Sharpe, 1999). For example, Oliver and Wilkinson (1992) identify low trade union strength (in other words, low level of labour dispute) as facilitating the diffusion of new work systems in Japanese subsidiaries in the UK. Furthermore, Sharpe (1999) points to the ability of firms to be highly selective with regard to their workforce (whereby skills can be developed in-house) on a greenfield site with high Japanese inward investment. It is suggested that high levels of foreign direct investment (FDI) familiarize workers in a region with the practices to be introduced (ibid.). Moreover, there is a strong network to support the adoption of 'new' systems. The brownfield site in Sharpe's research presents an unsupportive context, characterized by a declining traditional manufacturing region, low inward investment, a high level of industrial dispute and a heterogeneous workforce in terms of previous work experience, for the internalization of 'new' work practices. There is resistance to new methods of work and shop floor practices. Similarly, Oliver and Wilkinson (1992, p. 55) show that 'trade unions increase the scope for demarcation disputes, greatly hindering acceptance of change and flexible labour deployment within the company.'

Consequently, one can expect the degree of internalization of Japanese knowledge-driven work systems to be high where there is a favourable local institutional context characterized by a non-unionized labour market, and location on a greenfield site in an area with a strong service sector (where labour can be expected to be relatively free of preconceived ideas in manufacturing, and more easily indoctrinated in new ways of operating). Similarly, one would expect a large supply of unskilled workers in a given area to be conducive to the internalization of alternative work systems as workers would not be embedded in a tradition of manufacturing that can prove to be difficult to change. For example, Sharpe (1997, p. 186) notes that 'the possibility of starting with a new workforce, with comparatively less experience of factory work including middle-aged women and young workers recently out of school, with fewer preconceptions, [can allow] the introduction of initiatives with comparatively less resistance and fear by the workers.' In contrast, where there is an unfavourable local institutional context characterized by a unionized labour market, a small supply of unskilled workforce and location on a brownfield site in a centre for manufacturing, one can expect the degree of internalization of Japanese knowledge-driven work

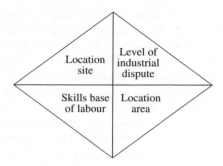

*Figure 1.2   Key local institutional characteristics that are likely to have an
impact on the diffusion of work systems*

systems to be low (see Figure 1.2 for a graphic representation of the key local
institutional characteristics that can have an impact on work systems
diffusion).

Key organizational characteristics

The nature of organizational characteristics, such as the size and age of the
company, are likely to affect the diffusion of Japanese knowledge-driven
work systems (see Lincoln and Kalleberg, 1990).[12] For instance, large organizations can offer more benefits than smaller enterprises, and this can
explain the high level of implementation of new practices. Similarly, the
longer the affiliate company is in operation, the more familiar are the
employees likely to become with the new work systems.

The nature of work systems can be an important factor in the degree to
which practices are diffused. The nature of work systems is conceptualized
in this study as structural, cultural, control-related and technological. The
four types of work systems are selected in such a way that a comprehensive
account of the phenomenon under investigation is provided. The diffusion
of organizational structures is defined here as a shift to team structure, that
is, to a structural environment created for employees to participate through
teams. Organizational structures are seen as having an effect on the work
attitudes of individual employees (see Lincoln and Kalleberg, 1990).

Cultural work systems are defined in this study as the values and norms
(Dacin et al., 1999) that constitute the philosophies which underlie the technical and structural elements of continuous improvement schemes such as
attention to detail and efforts committed to training. Chatman and Jehn
(1994) specify respect for people, detail and team orientation as some of the
values composing organizational culture. Cultural practices include internal training and small group activities and the underlying principles of

valuing the details of work, stressing quality, formalizing work stages and demanding high levels of task-related discipline, generally associated with Japanese management, and 'observed in many overseas subsidiaries of Japanese multinational corporations' (Dedoussis, 1995: 735). For example, training can be the core element of Japanese employees' high levels of commitment to continuous improvement activities (see for example Cutcher-Gershenfeld et al., 1998).

The degree of compatibility between values of the source firm and those of the adopter firm can be expected to have a positive impact on the diffusion process. Focusing on the adopter, it is suggested here that since the diffusion of work systems is typically associated with learning, change and innovation, the cultural orientation of the adopter towards learning, innovation and change are likely to result in a more positive attitude towards the diffusion process (see Kostova, 1999).

The willingness of employees to accept alternative work systems can have an impact on the diffusion process (Mathieu and Zajac, 1990). This is labeled here as the attitude of employees towards the work systems of the source firm. Specifically, it is the commitment, or the sense of ownership, which various groups within the adopter firm display towards quality improvement schemes. It is recognized here that employees play a major role in the internalization of 'new' work systems at the adopter end. For example, Takeuchi (1981) argues that the contribution of lower levels in the organizational hierarchy to the improvement of overall product quality has been very important in the overall strength of Japanese business activity. Furthermore, Casper (2000: 903) argues that medium levels of employee motivation, or a 'hold-up' problem, are highly likely in extremely competitive, demanding and time-intensive work environments, such as therapeutics. The situation is claimed to be even worse in firms that emphasize long-term relational contracts and engage in technological progress in a cumulative manner to generate firm-specific knowledge. It is proposed in the present study that high levels of commitment displayed by employees are likely to be favourable to the internalization of knowledge-driven work systems. By contrast, where the willingness of employees to accept alternative work systems is low, the internalization of these systems would be expected to be low.

Thus, it is proposed here that the degree of implementation and internalization of Japanese knowledge-driven work systems can be affected by the cultural nature of the diffused practices.

The control-related system is defined here as the degree of Japanese involvement in strategic decisions and operations, as well as hands-on management in the host or adopter company. This definition is based on Doz and Prahalad's (1984) argument that a partner's influence on a joint

venture's strategy formulation and implementation is a better measure of
control in circumstances where local firms depend highly on a foreign
partner's technology and marketing methods. Such involvement has implications for the adopter firm's perception of a power exercise by the source
company. The role of management or management intervention is crucial
in shaping that perception. Managers can act as a medium for acquiring
and encoding timely information. Their strategic and operational aims and
the way those aims are met (hands-on or hands-off) can have an impact on
the extent to which work systems are diffused. For example, a high level of
direct involvement in the development of employment skills in Japan tends
to influence the involvement of workers in innovative strategies positively
(Whitley, 2000b). Furthermore, studies of innovation processes show that
specialized personnel such as 'technological gatekeepers' have a significant
effect on the diffusion of knowledge between organizations (see for
example Inkpen and Dinur, 1998). Consequently, it is proposed here that
the degree to which Japanese work systems are put to use and accepted is
likely to be influenced by the control-related systems that are diffused.

It should be noted that high levels of control could result in a widespread
implementation of the source company's work systems but not necessarily
lead to a high level of internalization. As Kostova (1999: 319) argues,

> when the single motive for the transfer of a practice is to achieve legitimacy with,
> and approval by, the parent company, the employees at the recipient unit will go
> on to develop positive attitudes toward the practice. Thus, dependence will have
> effect on implementation but not on internalization.

Ideas or know-how about practices can be diffused only when such practices are actually perceived and realized by local employees (Abo, 1992).

A number of studies within the 'Japanization' literature point to
worker resistance in response to the power exercised by Japanese expatriate management in the diffusion of work systems (for example
Taylor et al., 1994; Delbridge, 1998). For example, workers can 'survive'
the system (that is, attempt to distance themselves from management by,
for example, not wearing the uniform and avoiding overtime), 'moder-
ate' the system (that is, attempt to secure some control over work such
as the speed), and 'beat' the system (that is, secure significant counter-
control in relation to the management system and actively to challenge
managerial prerogatives) (Delbridge, 1998). The worker response to a
power exercise can in part reflect the degree to which workers have internalized 'new' work systems.

Technological practices refer to advanced production systems technology
that is needed for the efficient running of assembly lines and technical
systems. Lack of such technology can be an impediment to delivering

efficiency improvements (see for example Boyer, 1998). Technology diffusion is seen as essential for the design and development of new models (see for example Chung, 1998). For instance, Hyundai relied on technology diffusion and styling concepts from Mitsubishi in order to reduce its lead time on model development (ibid., p. 171). The adoption of computer aided design/computer aided manufacturing (CAD/CAM) at Hyundai reduced expenditures on new model development by around 20 per cent by cutting work in progress. A skilful blend of people, business processes and technology can facilitate the implementation of Japanese work systems. This is based on the assumption that the diffusion process is related to group responsiveness, organizational characteristics and institutional characteristics such as employment systems, labour markets and organizational structure (Hedlund, 1994). Consequently, it is proposed here that technological practices can also have an effect on the diffusion of Japanese knowledge-driven work systems.

In the present study, cultural and control-related systems are taken as largely intangible,[13] tacit systems, whilst structural and technological systems are seen as representing largely tangible, explicit systems (see the section on the 'objectified and context-dependent views of work systems diffusion' for a conceptualization of tacit and explicit systems). This is in line with the distinction drawn by Brannen et al. (1999, p. 124) between the ' "hard side" [or the hardware] of the production system – the equipment, technical process flow (such as heat treat and machining), automation and flexible assembly' and the 'soft side', or the software, of the production system, such as a system of quality assurance, a clean and orderly workplace and well maintained equipment wherever possible. The software of the production system, in this context, refers to processes that are heavily people-dependent: that is of high system embeddedness. For example, 'In Japanese car plants people are still playing key roles at many levels' (Abo, 1992, p. 171). The plant level people are expected to have the ability to understand the linked processes before and after their own jobs and to be involved in attending to the machines, as well as the products handled by them. In other words, processes that are more or less tightly integrated with other technical and social systems are seen as being highly contextualized or of high tacitness. Tacit work systems in this study are operationalized as the intangible foundation of continuous improvement schemes, such as discipline, trust, team spirit and participation. By contrast, processes that can easily be detached from their context of formation are characterized in this study as highly objectified, to the extent that they are low in system embeddedness and reflect a large explicit knowledge base. Explicit work practices in the present study are operationalized as the tangible foundation of continuous improvement schemes, such as team-based organizational structure and technology.

It is proposed in the present study (in support of the propositions that are formulated in Chapter Two) that an emphasis on the cultural and control-related work systems, as defined here, can be favourable to the internalization of knowledge-driven work systems, as it would aid in diffusing the original meaning of the source company's work systems. The association of an exercise of control with the internalization of work systems is based on the argument that the Japanese tend to exercise implicit forms of control (that is, social investment that extends well beyond hierarchical principles) that may be less resisted by employees than explicit forms of control such as direct supervision (see for example McMillan, 1996). Furthermore, 'deliberate efforts to build trust, promote behavioural norms and information networks that lead to co-operation, consensus and a sense of collective vision in the Japanese corporation' (ibid., p. 214) can result in a high level of internalization of knowledge-driven work systems. By contrast, an emphasis on the structural and technological work systems, as defined here, can be unfavourable to the internalization of knowledge-driven work systems. The focus on the tangible features of alternative work systems can undercut people's motivation to commit themselves to alternative ways of working (see for example Cutcher-Gershenfeld et al., 1998).

As a whole, the knowledge-driven work systems in this study can be influenced by (i) the differences in national institutional context (that is, the degree of compatibility of structural and cultural legacies) between source and adopter companies; (ii) the labour market and inward investment patterns within the local institutional context and (iii) the organizational characteristics of the adopter firm, nature of the diffused work systems and adopting teams' perceived value of and commitment to the work systems.

Summary of the Analytic Framework

In the previous sections of this chapter, the key attributes of work systems diffusion and relevant key national and local institutional and organizational characteristics (which were presented as the building blocks of the analytic framework) that are likely to influence the diffusion process were identified and discussed. These building blocks are integrated into a single analytic framework (see Figure 1.3). This framework, in turn, is used to formulate five propositions in Chapter Two.

Figure 1.3 shows the impact of the key national institutional, local institutional and organizational characteristics on the degree of implementation and internalization of work systems. The structural elements, such as the type of capitalist system, location site, nature of diffused work systems and attitudes of employees towards the work systems of the source firm, are complemented with a process element, that is the process of internalizing work

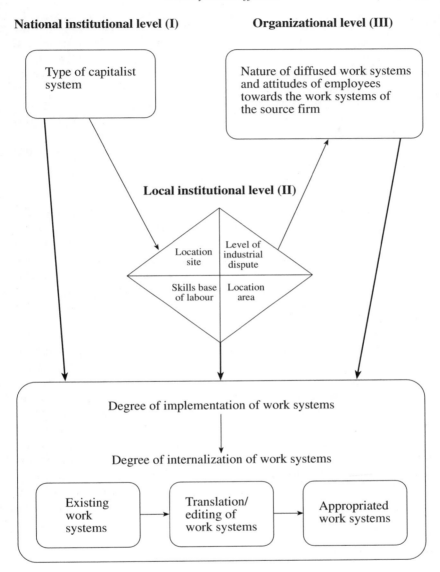

National institutional level (I)

Type of capitalist system

Organizational level (III)

Nature of diffused work systems and attitudes of employees towards the work systems of the source firm

Local institutional level (II)

Location site

Level of industrial dispute

Skills base of labour

Location area

Degree of implementation of work systems

Degree of internalization of work systems

Existing work systems

Translation/ editing of work systems

Appropriated work systems

Note: I, II and III are nested levels descending from the national through local institutional to the organizational level. I represents the highest level in the hierarchy and III represents the lowest.

Figure 1.3   Analytic framework

systems. It is proposed in this figure that the institutional variation at the national and regional levels can have an impact on the implementation and internalization of work systems. Similarly, at the organizational level, the nature of work systems that are diffused can positively or negatively influence the process whereby work systems are implemented and internalized.

The nature and the likely influence of key institutional and organizational characteristics have been addressed separately in this chapter, but it should be emphasized that it is their combined impact that needs to be taken into account for an analysis of the diffusion of work systems. Moreover, the likely influence of the suggested characteristics should not be taken as a straightjacket for the analysis. Rather, the figure serves as a schema for data analysis.

The application of the framework in a comparative analysis implies the following steps. First, data are gathered on the structural and cultural legacies of different countries (the UK and Japan). Then, the characteristics of each local institution are determined. Next, the attributes of work systems, including the nature of practices in each firm, are identified. This is followed by the exploration of employee attitudes towards alternative work systems. Finally, the elements in the framework are analysed in connection with each other, and the key (national and local) institutional and organizational characteristics are compared and contrasted to gain insights into the link between these characteristics and the extents of implementation and internalization. The application of the framework is discussed in the following chapter.

In sum, the historical neo-institutional perspective is refined in the following manner. First, the processes that underlie the implementation and internalization of work systems, acknowledging the role of actors, are made explicit. Second, detailed specifications of the implementation and internalization processes at the organizational level are called for in support of an analysis at the national level. Third, local institutional characteristics are taken into account in the operationalization of institutional variation across firms.

4.   SUMMARY

In this chapter, the concept of 'work systems' is defined and discussed. Work systems are understood as driven by people's knowledge, ideas and suggestions and founded on harnessing knowledge at the point where products are made and services are delivered. Both the structural and processual aspects of work systems are addressed.

On the basis of a review of comparative research approaches, specifically the labour process and lean production perspectives within the 'Japaniza-tion' literature, the user-oriented perspective within the innovation processes literature and the historical neo-institutional perspective within the neo-institutional literature, it has been indicated that the diffusion of work systems is influenced by the host country's legitimated structures and cul-tural understandings. Research concerning the institutional embeddedness of work systems has been discussed with particular reference to Whitley's divergent capitalisms view within the historical neo-institutionalist outlook on diffusion of work systems. From the six types of ideal business systems (fragmented, coordinated industrial district, compartmentalized, state organized, collaborative and highly coordinated), the present study focuses on the 'highly coordinated' and 'compartmentalized' business environ-ments, which reflect the Japanese and UK contexts respectively. It is argued in this chapter that nationally distinct societal environments of highly coor-dinated business systems allow for limited diffusability of work systems to other institutional environments. By contrast, competences of compart-mentalized business systems tend to be more mobile across borders owing to the absence of obligational ties to other actors in such systems. The impact of key national and local institutional and organizational charac-teristics on the diffusion process is discussed in an effort to construct an ana-lytic framework that can guide the present study.

NOTES

1. After all, as Blackler (1995: 1026) contends, '*all* individuals and *all* organizations, not just so-called "knowledge workers" or "knowledge organizations", are knowledgeable'.
2. The concept of 'diffusion of work systems' is used intentionally here to suggest that there is more to knowledge sharing within a firm than a transfer based on a functionalist com-munication model across firms. This will be further discussed in the section on 'the attrib-utes of work systems diffusion'.
3. Hence, the lean production perspective is also labelled as the technological/rational per-spective by some (such as Oliver and Wilkinson, 1992).
4. Although this research does not focus on an innovation, arguments drawn from the studies on innovation processes can be enlightening from the point of view of work systems diffusion.
5. Once institutionalized, governing rules tend to persist 'because they become integrated with wider economic institutions and ways of thinking' (Dobbin, 1995, p. 280).
6. Radical change is not incorporated into historical neo-institutionalism. Rather, this per-spective acknowledges the possibility that historical accidents or unanticipated develop-ments may occur with heavy reliance on path-dependent behaviour (Djelic, 1999). By the same token, Powell (1991, p. 193) argues that 'path-dependent models suggest that insti-tutional arrangements are not likely to be flexible; they cannot change rapidly in response to perturbations in the environment.' Hence, the rational choice neo-institutional assumption of reacting to, rather than enacting, the environment prevails to a degree in historical neo-institutionalism.
7. Research on Japanese overseas plants demonstrates that highly coordinated systems

'encourage domestic partners to establish subsidiaries in the same locations so that they can share risks with them and rely on established relationships to reduce uncertainty in the new environment' (Whitley, 1999c, p. 18).

8. Formal institutions in compartmentalized business environments 'tend to be organized into discrete spheres of influence with little co-ordination between them' (Whitley, 2000a, p. 8).

9. Polycentric strategy refers to the adoption of a system that conforms to local practices (Rosenzweig and Nohria, 1994).

10. The analytic distinction between highly coordinated and compartmentalized business systems in its link to the degree to which work systems are internalized will aid in the formulation of propositions in Chapter Two.

11. The separation of control and local adaptation activities is difficult where the knowledge diffused is highly tacit (Kogut and Zander, 1993).

12. The age of a company is not necessarily related to its location on a brownfield or a greenfield site. For example, a company on a brownfield site may be younger than one on a greenfield site.

13. Control-related systems are also seen as intangible owing to the reliance of the Japanese on networks of interdependence rather than formal sets of rules for surveillance (see for example Fucini and Fucini, 1990).

2.   The double embeddedness barrier

In this chapter, the application of the analytic framework, constructed in Chapter One, is discussed. The process of work systems diffusion is examined within Anglo-Japanese collaborations. The Japanese and UK contexts are discussed as nationally distinct social settings with specific organizational structural and cultural legacies. For this purpose, detailed descriptions are provided for each country relating to the nature of HRM systems or employment practices, such as the following: reward systems and employee governance, workplace relations and task organization and control or structural forms. The variation in the structural and cultural legacies between the two countries is shown to hinder the diffusion of 'new' work systems. A discussion of the institutional limits to the diffusion of work systems at the national level is followed by an outline of the difference in emphasis placed on tacit and explicit knowledge between Japan and the UK. The resulting insights on work systems diffusion are related to the analytic framework to fomulate a set of propositions with regard to the influence of institutional and organizational characteristics on the implementation and internalization of knowledge-driven work systems.

1.   LIMITS TO DIFFUSION OF WORK SYSTEMS

As was discussed in Chapter One, the diffusion of work systems can be influenced by the variation in the institutional settings of the source and adopter firms. This section discusses the difficulty in the diffusion of work systems, specifically from the Japanese context to that of the UK. The present study conceptualizes two levels of embeddedness in explaining the difficulty in the diffusion of work systems: one at the macro level and the other at the micro level. Macro-level embeddedness addresses the nationally distinct characteristics of social institutions, such as the legitimacy of Japanese and UK business systems, including structural characteristics of organizations and HRM systems. Micro-level embeddedness addresses the emphasis on the tacit nature of the diffused work systems. These are considered next.

Embeddedness at the National Level: Structural Legacies of Organizations

Organizational structural legacies of Japan

Dominant practices of firms in relation to work systems, reward systems and employee governance in Japan combine to form distinctive configurations. The presumed commitment and motivation advantage enjoyed by Japanese manufacturers over their Anglo-Saxon counterparts is said to emerge from a distinctive set of organizational structures and employment systems that characterize the Japanese workplace (Lincoln and Kalleberg, 1990). Bureaucracy and paternalism are synthesized (Clark, 1979; Hill, 1981) and welfare corporatism is advocated (Dore, 1973). This is also viewed as a combination of 'learning bureaucracy' and 'democratic Taylorism' (Adler, 1992). The highly coordinated national business system of Japan nurtures collectivist values and tightly knit networks that encourage low strike activity, absenteeism and turnover (Yoshimura and Anderson, 1997). The norms governing trust and authority relations promote close links between managers and employees and allow for greater informal participation in decisions compared with 'Western' plants (see Lincoln and Kalleberg, 1990).

According to Morgan et al. (2000a, p. 11), 'Japanese firms in general tend to be the least diversified; they concentrate on a particular range of skills and competences around specific technologies and markets.' Their subsidiaries are highly integrated into the Japanese headquarters. Unlike Anglo-Saxon firms' preference for 'flat' organizational structures and greater diversification, Japanese organizations are seen as having thickly populated vertical hierarchies and proliferating work units, which break up occupational and class loyalties while encouraging the formation of organization-wide cohesive bonds (Besser, 1996; Liker et al., 1999).

A key feature of Japanese firms is believed to be their commitment to small group activities (Cole, 1979). Team-level sharing, as in quality circles and new model changeover teams, is said to strengthen factory knowledge-creation capabilities (see Fruin's (1997) study of knowledge works at Toshiba). It is argued that these activities enhance knowledge-sharing through 'socialization' (Nonaka and Takeuchi, 1995),[1] and create a 'sense of belonging, involvement and participation' (Liker et al., 1999, p.11). However, it should be noted that this participation is more operational than strategic (see for example Turnbull and Delbridge, 1994; Delbridge, 1995). Such involvement takes place within a context of high vertical hierarchy, formalization and standardization in production systems (Yoshino, 1968). This type of hierarchy differs from that found in British firms. Liker et al. (1999) argue that there is relatively limited coercive rationale that produces efficiency at the expense of worker commitment, flexibility and improvement momentum in the Japanese hierarchy.[2]

Overall, as was presented in Chapter One, the Japanese national business system is characterized by a considerably reliable legal system, coordinating and developing state, bank (credit)-based financial system, limited public training system, highly paternalist authority and limited union strength (Whitley, 1999b; 2000a).

Organizational structural legacies of the UK
In contrast to a synthesis of bureaucracy and paternalism commonly observed in Japan, there are 'fewer supervisory contacts, less worker control, and a poorer quality of supervisory and co-worker relations in the West' (Lincoln and Kalleberg, 1990, p. 233). It is argued that the structural differentiation or pronounced differences among managers, supervisors and workers do not encourage teamwork. The form of bureaucracy found in traditional UK firms is seen as different from that of Japanese firms, in that it is designed for the purpose of control. Its procedures and standards serve to control performance standards. Organizational structures in the UK business system tend to be marked by 'flatter and fatter' hierarchies owing, in part, to the fact that promotion and pay are based on merit (Besser, 1996).[3] The business behaviour, based on individualism in the UK (Casson et al., 1996), is likely to lead to adverse competitive behaviour among firms. Management's desire for control over many key operating decisions and arm's length relations between actors in Britain have reinforced a basic conflict model of the workplace in which strike activity, absenteeism and turnover have been common occurrences (see Lane, 1996; McMillan, 1996).

Overall, as was presented in Chapter One, the UK national business system is characterized by a reliable legal system, regulative state, financial system based on a capital market, weak public training system, low paternalistic authority and low union strength (Whitley (1999b, p. 61); see Table 2.1 for a comparison of the types of business environments in Japan and the UK).

Embeddedness at the National Level: Cultural Legacies of Organizations

Organizational cultural legacies of Japan
Some of the work processes which differentiate East Asian work systems from many continental European ones are task specialization, degree of worker discretion, degree of managerial control, degree of separation and segmentation between managers and workers, and degree of employer commitment to employment security (Whitley, 1999b).[4]

It is argued that the Japanese management system allows considerable independence to individuals or work groups as to how work is conducted, and tasks are usually more broadly defined (Pascale and Athos, 1986;

*Table 2.1   The national institutional features associated with types of
            business systems in Japan and the UK*

Types of business system/Key features	Highly coordinated (such as Japan)	Compartmentalized (such as the UK)
Authority relations	Highly paternalist	Contractual
State	Coordinating and developing	Regulative
Legal system	Considerably reliable	Reliable
Financial system	Bank (Credit)-based	Capital market
Public training system	Limited	Weak
Union strength	Limited	Low

Source: Adapted from Whitley (2000a and 1999b, p. 60)

Fukuda, 1987; Kenney and Florida, 1995). There is an effort to secure
'enhanced leverage over effort and worker compliance to boot' (Danford,
1998, p. 41). The characteristic of 'groupism' (Wilms et al., 1994) is widely
seen as conducive to the effective running of Kaizen systems (Tolich et al.,
1999). The education system in Japan is said to provide 'little or no tradition of independent craft or skill, so companies take on employees and
train them up, in-house, entirely according to their own needs' (George and
Levie, 1984, p. 26). It is not only the leaders and facilitators of the quality
control (QC) process who are trained. In Japan, years rather than hours are
spent on the training of QC members.

Although Japanese workers in large organizations may have some discretion over performance, they 'have very little say in what tasks they do or
the conditions under which they do them' (Whitley, 1999b, p. 90). Unlike
the Taylorized system observed in the UK (Lane, 1996), the 'paternalistic
delegated responsibility' system in Japan offers low reward differentials and
segmentation between managers and workers. The world image of the
Japanese in the 1980s rested on, and to a large degree still rests on, 'commitment, identification, and loyalty Japanese employees exhibit toward
their firms, low rates of industrial conflict, absenteeism and turnover combined with higher worker productivity and production quality' (Lincoln
and Kalleberg, 1990, p. 738). These characteristics may prove difficult to
replicate in the UK context, which is characterized by adversarial relations
between management and workers.

It is a known practice for 'Japanese employers to set out to build organizational cultures, involving high levels of worker commitment, and flexibility'
(Warner, 1994: 510). This model is based on three pillars: seniority wages
(*nenko*), lifetime employment (*shunshi koyo*)[5] and enterprise unionism
(*kigyobetsu rodo kumiai*) (Morris and Wilkinson, 1995). Japanese manage-

ment principles that typically emphasize the key objectives of quality and flexibility, long-term growth (Sullivan et al., 1981), market share, employment security and close, trust-based relations with suppliers, customers and financers (Lillrank, 1995) stand on these pillars.

The Japanese system of corporate management, such as employment stability and strong employee identification with the company, is seen as combining low levels of job fragmentation, high employer commitment to employment security, considerable worker involvement and managerial control of work organization and relatively low separation of manager from workers (Whitley, 1999b, p. 92). 'The practices ascribed to Japanese management are seen in a variety of non-Japanese organizations, but are more normatively accepted in Japan' (Besser, 1996, p. 11). Although Japan's employment practices are currently in a state of change, triggered by the Asian financial crisis of the early 1990s, they are still seen as having positive implications for participative, hands-on management; commitment to continuous improvement activities, team work and on-the-job training. There are few indicators that speak of any 'radical transformation' in the Japanese workplace at this point (Dirks et al., 2000). Proposals to rejuvenate Japanese firms by introducing individual initiative, clarity in job descriptions, multi-track personnel systems with distinct hiring, remuneration, welfare, training and promotion schemes serve as symbols and metaphors, rather than blueprints, that create tension or conflict between what is and what would or should be. Similarly, Porter et al. (2000, p. 17) contend that 'there have been some calls for restructuring especially in the financial sector but no consensus on what the restructuring should look like.'

Organizational cultural legacies of the UK

In comparison with the human resource practices observed in Japan, the UK system of HRM is less homogeneous across industries and sector. Nonetheless, two general features of the system can be outlined when making comparisons with other countries: first, industrial relations in the UK have been adversarial[6] and second, employment security is low (McMillan, 1996). Unions in Britain have traditionally had only marginal influence over hiring and firing practices (Lane, 1996). Lower employment security in Britain (Whitley, 1999b) is connected to lower investment in skills development by UK firms (Sako, 1992) and the lack of a lifetime relationship with employees (Ho, 1993; Scarbrough and Terry, 1998). 'The training system is more weakly institutionalized and standardized across industrial sectors' (Whitley, 1997, p. 256). British deficiencies in skills training have negative implications for technical cooperation and trust. Given British managers' low level of formal education in comparison to those in strongly institutionalized contexts, such as that of Germany (Lane, 1996), there are frequent transfers for promotion between firms, as well as changing far more between functional specialisms within firms. In addition, the educational level of workers has been such that the expectations of workers have been largely economic rather than social (McMillan, 1996). High managerial control and low worker discretion or involvement are seen as creating 'them and us attitude problems' (Oliver and Wilkinson, 1992, p. 186). With the availability of low skill workers, management hierarchy has been enhanced and the ideological framework of 'them and us' has been reinforced. Such an ideological framework can limit the extent to which commitment among UK workers can be attained.

According to Whitley (1999b, p. 92), the UK work system can be dominantly identified as a 'Taylorist' one that 'combines high levels of job fragmentation, managerial control over task performance and work organization, strong manager-worker separation, and low employer commitment to employment security' (see Table 2.2 for a comparison of the types of work systems in Japan and the UK).

Table 2.2   Types of work systems in Japan and the UK

Characteristics	Paternalist (such as Japan)	Taylorist (such as the UK)
Task fragmentation	Low	High
Worker discretion and involvement	Considerable	Low
Managerial control of work organization	Considerable	High
Separation of manager from workers	Variable	High
Employer commitment to employment security for core workforce	High	Low

Source: Adapted from Whitley (1999b, p. 92)

As with the categorization of business systems characteristics in Table 2.1, only dominant characteristics of work systems are highlighted in Table 2.2. Although the operationalization of the 'paternalist' and 'Taylorist' typologies is static, it is useful in providing a general picture, in relative terms, of the dominant forms of work systems in different national contexts.

Embeddedness at the Organizational Level

There is a difference between Japan and the UK in the emphasis placed on explicit and tacit knowledge. Work systems are considered as highly tacit in Japan, whilst they are assumed to be of lower tacitness in the UK (see Inkpen and Dinur, 1998). The basis for this claim rests on the argument that

'Western firms lose much of their potential for knowledge creation by overemphasizing explicit knowledge and the development of complex managerial hierarchies, systems and standardization' (Inkpen and Dinur, 1998: 457; Hedlund and Nonaka, 1993). The emphasis on tacit knowledge in the UK is overshadowed by the importance given to more easily transferable explicit knowledge (Takeuchi, 1998). This is partly evidenced by the Anglo-Saxon firms' propensity to jump on fashion bandwagons (see for example Abrahamson, 1996).

Emphasis on tacit knowledge in Japan

Japan tends to emphasize tacit knowledge and the process of creating new knowledge with the involvement of everyone (Nonaka and Takeuchi, 1995; Takeuchi, 1998). In this context, communication is seen as an integral part of the knowledge diffusion process. Japanese firms tend to focus on the 'soft' dimension of management that is skills, staff, style and superordinate goals, rather than strategy, structure and systems (Pascale and Athos, 1986). Similarly, Nonaka and Johansson (1985) argue that it is 'natural' for Japanese firms to demonstrate an environment of organizational learning owing to Japanese management's consensus decision-making process that facilitates knowledge-sharing and on-the-job and continuous education. Many of the knowledge diffusion issues 'come down to finding effective ways to let people talk and listen to one another' (Davenport and Prusak, 1998, p.88), and this tends to be provided by the Japanese context. According to Takeuchi (1998), Japanese emphasis rests on the importance it places on the 'whole personality', rather than the mind alone. There is no dualism between the knower and the known.[7] Hence, there is an attempt to keep the human element of knowledge production alive.[8] There is an organizational, rather than a market, orientation to skills development in Japan. There are rules and hierarchies governing employer–employee relations within a plant or corporation. Consequently, skills profiles are developed internally through corporate training policies. 'A high degree of homogeneity of markets and skills, together with distinctive employment practices, traditionally have linked together to facilitate high commitment to the enterprise as a whole' (Sharpe, 2001, p.197). Internally developed incentives for training, commitment and turnover render work systems in Japan highly tacit.

Given the emphasis on tacit knowledge, it can be argued that Japanese work systems are more difficult to diffuse to a setting that emphasizes explicit knowledge. Hybrid solutions are common where Japanese belief systems, which are not readily compatible with those of compartmentalized business systems, are diffused to Anglo-Saxon contexts (see Taylor et al., 1994; Mair, 1998). QCs, JIT delivery, teams and suggestion programmes, which are interdependent within an entire system of a strongly institution-alized context can produce vastly different results when taken out of context.

Emphasis on explicit knowledge in the UK

In comparison with the Japanese, UK managers tend to focus more on explicit knowledge that can be measured and managed by a selected few who carry out knowledge initiatives (Takeuchi, 1998). 'There is a long philosophical tradition in the West of valuing precise, conceptual knowl-edge and systematic sciences, which can be traced back to Descartes' (ibid., p. 6). This is the type of knowledge that can be processed by a computer, transmitted electronically and stored in databases and, hence, is equated with information technology in the 'West' (Spender, 1996). Its diffusion can be characterized as an objectified mode of knowledge communication (see Scarbrough, 1995). The focus on this mode of communication in the UK is in contrast with Japan's emphasis on informal, 'on-the-job' knowledge,[9] stored in people's brains, found in networks of social relations, and com-municated in a sedimented mode. The emphasis of UK firms on explicit knowledge (see Hedlund and Nonaka, 1993; Boisot, 1995) reflects the bias towards the easier of the two kinds of knowledge to measure, control and process, as such knowledge is not categorized as highly subjective, personal and cognitive that requires interaction through the actions of individuals. By contrast, knowledge in the UK tends not to be created by the 'interac-tion of frontline employees, middle managers and top management with middle managers in line positions playing the key synthesizing role' (Takeuchi, 1998, p. 9). Knowledge is, rather, managed by a few key players in staff positions, including information processing or internal consultancy. This, in line with the Cartesian separation between mind and body, reflects the goal of economizing on 'immediate truth-seeking, identity-location and affirmation, . . . universalism, unambiguity, logical precision, rightness, method and principles as the guiding axioms of good managerial practice' (Chia, 2000, p. 7). Chia argues that such an approach cannot capture the dynamic and richly textured nuances of social exchanges in Eastern set-tings. Firms under highly competitive external labour markets tend not to invest in general training due to the risk that workers can leave the firm. Rather, they pay trained individuals market wages in a competitive labour market (McMillan, 1996). Consequently, markets that are governed by supply/demand conditions in the economy at large encourage selection and screening policies that do not have to be too sophisticated. A worker can be laid off or may transfer if the economic contract turns out to be unfavourable. The external labour market approach to skills development renders work systems in the UK highly explicit.

The emphasis on explicit or objectified mode of knowledge in the UK business system is consistent with the work systems characteristics of Taylorist organizations. Explicit knowledge 'tends to generate a unified and predictable pattern of behaviour and output in organizations' (Lam, 1998: 10) that encourages high levels of managerial control and low levels of worker involvement in decisions. (This corresponds to the third characteristic in Table 2.2.) The codification of knowledge, or its abstraction from social networks, tends to reduce investment in personal interaction or sharing of tacit knowledge. This implies a 'high' separation of managers from workers in Taylorist organizations (see the fourth characteristic in Table 2.2). In line with the principles of Taylorism, complex social or team relationships tend to receive limited attention in the codification of workers' experiences, or formalization of work roles and procedures by UK firms. This renders the UK business system, in comparison to that of Japan, a weak institutional context.

The impact of the embeddedness of Japanese knowledge-driven work systems at the national institutional and organizational levels on their diffusability to the UK can be seen in Figure 2.1. This figure highlights the contrasting nature of the two levels of embeddedness between Japan and the UK.

It is assumed here that the nationally distinct nature of the institutional environment in which automotive manufacturing firms in Japan are embedded has facilitated the development of a highly coordinated structure and a paternalist culture. The 'strong institutional context' in Figure 2.1 represents the highly coordinated business system characterized by a network of mutual obligations and commitment. Within such a context, predominant economic relationships are paternalist and the sectors cohere strongly.

By contrast, the UK context is characterized by a compartmentalized structure and a Taylorist culture. The 'weak institutional context' in Figure 2.1 represents the compartmentalized business system characterized by work systems that are not strongly embedded in social networks of close cooperation and high interdependency. Predominant economic relationships are Taylorist. Such a system does not bear the institutional support necessary for a long-term orientation to developing competencies.

Figure 2.1 shows the diffusability of work systems from a strong institutional context, such as that of Japan, to a relatively weak one, such as that of the UK. The figure implies that work systems become *less diffusable* as they are moved from highly coordinated structural legacies and paternalist cultural legacies at the macro level,[10] and high knowledge tacitness at the organizational level in Japan to a context characterized by compartmentalized structural legacies and Taylorist cultural legacies at the macro level, and low knowledge tacitness (or high knowledge explicitness) at the micro level in the UK.

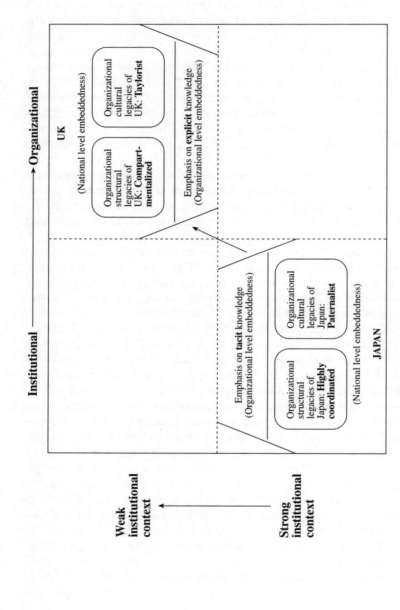

Source: Figure structure adapted from Inkpen and Dinur (1998: 457)

Figure 2.1 *The impact of national institutional and organizational levels on work systems diffusion*

2. PROPOSITIONS

The analytic framework constructed in Chapter One, complemented by the discussion in the above sections, forms the basis of the propositions on the influence of key institutional and organizational characteristics on the implementation and internalization of Japanese knowledge-driven work systems.

As was pointed out earlier (Section Three, Chapter One), favourable key characteristics are likely to have a positive impact on the degree of implementation and internalization. By contrast, if a firm is embedded in an environment with unfavourable key characteristics, identified as such in the literature review, a low degree of implementation and internalization of knowledge-driven work systems is expected to be observed. In Section One of this chapter, favourable and unfavourable key characteristics were discussed separately in their link to the degree of implementation and internalization of Japanese knowledge-driven work systems under the following headings: the influence of key institutional characteristics and the influence of key organizational characteristics. This discussion is summarized here in the form of two institutional settings that can be identified as contrasting in nature. In an attempt to formulate propositions, these institutional settings are taken to represent two extreme points of a scale, ranging from 'favourable' to 'unfavourable' (see Table 2.3). It should be noted that 'intermediate' settings can also prevail in between the two extremes.

On the basis of the scale in Table 2.3 that reflects the expected degree of implementation and internalization of Japanese knowledge-driven work systems in connection with a set of favourable and unfavourable key institutional and organizational characteristics, five propositions can be formulated. The first two propositions are formulated on the basis of two extreme points of the scale. The three remaining propositions reflect the institutional settings and degrees of implementation and internalization of Japanese knowledge-driven work systems that are likely to be found in between the two extremes.

Proposition 1

Affiliates of MNCs in highly institutionalized environments that are operating in unfavourable institutional settings overseas (as those delineated in Table 2.3) are likely to exhibit a low degree of implementation and internalization of MNC work systems.

Similarly, a second proposition can be made to reflect the opposite argument.

Table 2.3   *Contrasting institutional settings**

High degree of implementation and internalization of Japanese work systems	'Intermediate' institutional settings	Low degree of implementation and internalization of Japanese work systems
Favourable key characteristics		*Unfavourable key characteristics*
National institutional level		*National institutional level*
Highly coordinated structural legacy		Compartmentalized structural legacy
Paternalist cultural legacy		Taylorist cultural legacy
Local institutional level		*Local institutional level*
Location on a greenfield site		Location on a brownfield site
Location in a centre for service		Location in a centre for manufacturing
Large supply of unskilled workers		Small supply of unskilled workers
Low level of industrial dispute		High level of industrial dispute
Organizational level		*Organizational level*
Emphasis on tacit knowledge		Emphasis on explicit knowledge
Emphasis on cultural and control-related practices		Emphasis on structural and technological practices
High level of employee commitment		Low level of employee commitment

Note: *This scale bears two ideal extremes where all the suggested key characteristics are assumed to form a tightly knit coherent whole to represent two opposing institutional settings.

Proposition 2

Affiliates of MNCs in highly institutionalized environments that are operating in favourable institutional settings overseas (as those delineated in Table 2.3) are likely to exhibit a high degree of implementation and internalization of MNC work systems.

Propositions can also be made to take into account the less tightly knit institutional settings that may have an impact on the degree of implementation and internalization of MNC work systems.

Proposition 3

Affiliates of MNCs in highly institutionalized environments that are operating in settings in which unfavourable key institutional, and organizational characteristics are more dominant than the favourable ones are likely to exhibit a low degree of implementation and internalization of MNC work systems.

The counter-argument is as follows.

Proposition 4

Affiliates of MNCs in highly institutionalized environments that are operating in settings in which favourable key institutional and organizational characteristics are more dominant than the unfavourable ones are likely to exhibit a high degree of implementation and internalization of MNC work systems.

There is also the possibility that a high or low degree of implementation and internalization of work systems is attained in settings that lack the dominating effect of the favourable or unfavourable key institutional and organizational characteristics.

Proposition 5

An incoherent pattern of high and low degree of implementation and internalization is likely to develop in settings which lack key institutional and organizational characteristics that are favourable or unfavourable.

These five propositions further clarify the aim of the field study presented in Chapter Four.

3. SUMMARY

In this chapter, the limits to diffusion of work systems are discussed in terms of their embeddedness at the macro national and micro organizational levels. The variation in organizational structural and cultural legacies between Japan and the UK are argued to affect the diffusability of work systems. Similarly, the difference in emphasis placed on tacit and explicit knowledge between Japan and the UK is argued to have an impact on the extent to which work systems can be diffused. It is argued that work systems become less diffusable as they are moved from highly coordinated structural legacies and paternalist cultural legacies at the macro level, and high knowledge tacitness at the organizational level in Japan to a context characterized by compartmentalized structural legacies and Taylorist cultural legacies at the macro level, and high knowledge explicitness at the micro level in the UK. Five propositions are formulated on the basis of a scale ranging from favourable to unfavourable institutional settings and their impact on the degree of implementation and internalization of MNC work systems.

NOTES

1. This is illustrated by Matsushita's Home Bakery team. 'At Matsushita, team members apprenticed themselves to the head baker at Osaka International Hotel to capture the essence of kneading skill through bodily experience' (Nonaka and Takeuchi, 1995, p. 85).
2. In spite of arguments for the distinctive architectural features of Japanese firms, Japanese organizations are fundamentally not different in their multidivisional structural features from their European counterparts. Historically, similar to European firms, they displayed a clear, top-down structure organized around functions. With the 'presence of successful US multinationals, largely organized around the multidivisional structure' in Europe and the role of consulting firms, there was a spread in the multidivisional form in Britain (McMillan, 1996, p. 217). The shift to this structure was much slower in Japan. According to Suzuki (1980), only 56 per cent of the top 100 Japanese firms had adopted the divisional structure, as compared with the 72 per cent in Britain, by the mid-1960s. Nevertheless, 'similarities' in macro-organizational features in Japan and the UK are exposed to the influence of different traditions and interpersonal relations or meso-level organizational features. Hence, the way in which multidivisional structures operate in the two countries varies.
3. On the other hand, the Japanese management system is seen as upholding a seniority-based pay system as a means of developing core employees (Sako and Sato, 1997).
4. Please note that the discussion on organizational cultural legacies of Japan and the UK is structured along these five dimensions, which are labelled by Whitley (1999b) as 'characteristics of work systems'.
5. Lifetime employment is seen as having positive implications for skills development and labour turnover (see Dickens and Savage, 1988).
6. This is associated with the confrontational nature of management–worker relationships in the UK (see for example Maurice et al., 1980).
7. The different forms of knowledge in Japan and the 'West' tend to be dictated by the intellectual traditions of Zen Buddhism and Cartesian dualism (Takeuchi, 1998). The former is based on the principle of 'the oneness of the body and mind', whilst the latter is

founded on the argument that 'true knowledge can be obtained only by the mind, not the body' (ibid., p.7; also see discussion of East–West managerial mindsets in Chia, 2000).

8. This avoids the degeneration of knowledge production into a fad (see case studies in Scarbrough and Swan, 1999).

9. The 'gradualist' ideas derived from factory experiences exemplify this point well (see for example Hull et al., 1985). The use of the word 'gradualist' serves to distinguish between the 'incremental' innovation approach, adopted by, for instance, Japanese companies and the 'radical' or 'great-leap' innovation approach upheld generally by Anglo-Saxon companies (Imai, 1986).

10. Rosenzweig and Nohria (1994) claim that the greater the socio-cultural difference between MNCs (that is, the cultural distance between the parent company and the host country), the more likely it is for the local adaptation of, for instance, HRM practices to local interests and diversity. The authors argue that the method of founding, presence of expatriates and the extent of communication with the parent company can limit the adoption of parent companies' work systems.

PART II

Some empirical evidence

3. Research methodology

This chapter concerns the methodological aspects of the study presented here: that is, where and how the research project was carried out so as to arrive at answers to the central research question. The criteria used to select firms for the field study as well as the process of collecting and analysing data are addressed.

The study systematically compares three cases in the automotive sector – Teniki UK, Nissera UK and the Rover–Honda collaboration – to highlight the conditions for the implementation and internalization of Japanese work systems.

1. DATA COLLECTION

The Selection of Firms

Data were collected relating to the degree to which Japanese knowledge-driven work systems were put into practice and accepted at two UK subsidiary firms in the automotive manufacturing sector and a UK-based Anglo-Japanese technical collaboration between two major car manufacturers. The automotive sector lent itself to investigating the limits to diffusing 'Japanese best practices', for the UK automotive manufacturing sector was heavily influenced by Japanese investment, particularly in the late 1980s. The research sites were collected with the intention to include a brownfield subsidiary, a greenfield subsidiary and a technical collaboration site in an effort to address the need to incorporate the social context in which organizational practices are embedded.

Rover provided a good example of work systems diffusion whereby its claimed successful collaboration with Honda until 1995 created 'centres of excellence', or central specialism in the form of project teams that benefited from each other's experience (see Faulkner, 1995; Ohtani et al., 1997). The greenfield site, Nissera UK (a pseudonym), was claimed by managers to be a good example of a UK subsidiary firm that had successfully implemented Japanese work systems. The brownfield site, Teniki UK (another pseudonym), aimed to be more market-oriented and quality conscious by adopting Japanese work systems.[1] All of the three firms were examples of firms adopting Japanese continuous improvement schemes to make them work in the UK.

Firms involved in the study were selected according to specific criteria including the form of ownership, nature of diffused work systems, site and sector. Sites were selected to achieve variety in terms of aspects such as firm location and form of ownership. It should be noted that whilst demographic information on the cases is important for drawing conclusions, one must look beyond structural classifications to recognize each firm as representing a 'unique community of people who go about their business in a distinctive setting' (Cutcher-Gershenfeld et al., 1998, p. 20). The selection of the technical collaboration case – the Rover–Honda collaboration – was mainly based on Rover's long-standing relationship with a major Japanese car manufacturer, Honda. Honda was the most innovative Japanese manufacturer in the mid-1980s. It had the characteristic of a Japanese total quality control (TQC) attitude to manufacturing. The collaboration between Rover and Honda lent itself to research as there were intensive efforts to diffuse a TQC system to Rover. This research focused on the Rover 200/Honda Concerto (coded the R8/YY) project, as this constituted 'side-by-side' work rather than an 'arm's length' relationship, reflecting the similarity in goals and the learning from the previous collaborative projects (see Appendix I for a series of collaborative projects in the Rover–Honda relationship). This project was seen by Rover engineers and senior managers as the most successful project in terms of the degree of collaboration, quality and process improvement, problem resolution and learning benefits.

Table 3.1 lists the firms that were involved in this study. It presents information on their date of establishment, location, core business, size, form of ownership, nature of diffused work systems and sector. There was an attempt to standardize parameters across firms for a comparison along the lines of sector and nature of diffused practices. It is recognized in this study that variation in structural characteristics across the three cases, such as company size, can influence the degree to which work systems are implemented and internalized. However, an attempt is made here at highlighting the interaction between organizational members and the process of attaching meaning to alternative work systems.

Both of the subsidiary firms were roughly medium-sized (170 and 300 employees respectively). However, the third firm differed in terms of its number of employees, being a large-sized firm. Similarly, the time span from the year of initial investment to data collection, labelled here as company age, differed across the sites (being either three or 11 years). The literature suggests that different types of firms within the same industry behave in a dissimilar fashion (see for example Chesbrough, 1998). Hence,

Table 3.1 Firms involved in the study

Firm (in the order of data collection)	Year of acquisition/ commencement/ establishment	Site	Core business	Size (number of employees)	Form of ownership	Nature of diffused work systems	Sector
1 Teniki UK Parent: Teniki Ltd. in Japan	1996	Pre-existing culture (brownfield)	Car component assembly	Medium (170 in 1999)	Subsidiary	Continuous improvement schemes	Automotive manufacturing
2 Rover R8/YY project Partner: Honda Motor Corporation in Japan	1985 (the collaboration was launched in 1978)	Pre-existing culture (home of Britain's traditional car manufacturing base)	Automobile design, engineering and manufacture	Large (37,675 in 1985, ~39,000 in 1999)	Technical collaboration		
3 Nissera UK Parent: Nissera Ltd. in Japan	1988	New culture (greenfield)	Car component assembly	Medium (300 in 1999)	Subsidiary		

the likely impact that the differences in company size and age could have on the diffusion of Japanese knowledge-driven work systems was taken into account.

Nissera UK was similar to Teniki UK in terms of the form of ownership, company size, nature of diffused work systems and sector. However, in terms of company age (from investment to data collection), it was similar to the Rover–Honda collaboration site.[2] Although the Rover-Honda collaboration was larger than the two subsidiary firms in size and operated under a different form of ownership, it was similar to Teniki UK and Nissera UK in terms of the nature of diffused work systems and sector. The Rover case had a local institutional context that was similar to that of Teniki UK, particularly in terms of site location. Rover's similarity with Nissera UK was more in terms of both companies aspiring to be successful models of diffused Japanese work systems. While the selected companies could not be closely matched, the research procedure was subjected to adequacy or validity and reliability measures to attain a high level of consistency in data analysis.

As was discussed in Chapter One, multiple levels were addressed in this study to gain an integrated understanding into work systems diffusion. If the national context alone was addressed, then one would expect similar outcomes in the levels of internalization in each of the three cases. This would be to ignore any possible variation in the degree to which Japanese knowledge-driven work systems are internalized across firms located in the same sector within a single country.

Justification of a Comparative Study

A number of studies on knowledge diffusion are characterized by generalizations which are assumed to be universal but are in fact conditioned by the circumstances of time and place (see for example Rogers, 1983). For example, Rogers' (1983) work is seen as a somewhat prescriptive supply-side model that draws a linear relationship between the supplier and the user of knowledge to be 'transferred'. Knowledge in this context is objectified and manipulated for rapid 'transfer'.[3] His model, which is further developed by Clark and Staunton (1989), is criticized for ignoring the embeddedness of knowledge-driven work systems in complex ensembles of routines which may inhibit or enable the firms' ability to use diffused systems. The diffusion process is complex, involving political processes of the suppliers and the active involvement of the users. The context-bound nature of diffusion necessitates the acknowledgement of the institutional context that shapes the internalization of a practice in a new national system (Clark, 1987). To test whether one's explanatory arguments are context-bound, one should investigate experience in more than one environment. If the experience applies in a diversity of times and places, one may assume that one has identified a robust generalization. Otherwise, one needs to explore the situational characteristics that may explain the differences in outcomes that tend to persist, resisting pressures to converge (Hyman, 1998). This essentially serves as a means of teasing out macro institutional influences from the micro organizational effects.

Comparative research also has a potential role in identifying 'lessons'. For example, the appropriation of production and inventory control systems in the British context was modelled on the American vision, templates and artefacts and 'diffused through a strong presence of American suppliers (e.g. IBM) and major American consultancies (e.g. Arthur Anderson)' (Clark and Newell, 1993: 77). The key player in the diffusion of the system – the British Production and Inventory Control Society (BPICS) – was in fact a licensee of the American Society, APICS. A comparative study of the British and the US production and inventory control systems provided an opportunity to account for persistent differences. It also allowed for the acknowledgement of peculiarities of each national institutional context. Such an analysis falls into alignment with the neo-institutionalist arguments, which argue for the specificities of national institutional frameworks. A comparative study is also useful for saturating categories of incidents, for it provides the opportunity to maximize differences among groups. '[Theoretical] saturation can never be attained by studying one incident in one group' (Glaser and Strauss, 1967, p. 63).

This research focuses on an inter-firm comparison in a single national system with references drawn from the national context that serves as the supplier of alternative work systems. The comparative study seeks to establish and account for similarities and differences in the cases investigated. It is not a paired cross-national comparison, as the companies under study in Japan and the UK are not matched on age, size and technological advancement. Those in Japan constitute the parent or partner firms of the affiliate firms in the UK.

From a methodological standpoint, the comparative approach also aims to achieve the objective of testing and exploring the pervasiveness of uniqueness. 'Paradoxically, uniqueness can only be demonstrated through systematic comparison that differentiates a country from all others as a deviant case in a given universe' (Rose, 1991 in Hyman, 2001, p. 210). In other words, exceptionalism needs to be integrated through comparative analysis. Such an analysis also allows one to identify explanatory propositions in a systematic manner.

Within this study, there is a focus on comparing processes as well as institutional structures. One implication of this comparison is that elements of the given process, such as workers' response to alternative work systems, may be the same across countries despite institutional differences. Hyman (2001, pp. 215–16) argues that 'national institutions of interest representation are not appropriate units for comparative analysis, for they are differently constituted, differently experienced and differently set in motion according to specific national context.' Hence, the aim here is to highlight both macro institutional and micro organizational influences on the diffusion process across sites in a specific national context.

Doing a qualitative case study encompassing interviews and participant observation

The research is based on a qualitative case study of the contextual characteristics that influence firms' ability to adopt new ideas (see for example Hislop et al., 1998), drawing both on interviews and participant observation. Platt (1988) notes that one would use case studies when one deliberately wants to cover contextual conditions. Qualitative case studies enable one to carry out investigations where other methods such as experiments do not lend themselves to viewing the case from the perspective of those involved (Gillham, 2000). The interest in the present study is to carry out research into the processes leading to results rather than into the 'significance' of the results themselves. The study aims to explain through developing understanding rather than through predictive testing. As it focuses on the actions and taken-for-granted meanings of research participants, the researcher comes closer to, rather than removed from, the data. In line with Delbridge's (1998, p. 17) argument, the aim of this study is to seek in part 'detailed description of the reality of workplace relations and to relate these findings to contemporary theory and other studies of "empirical tendencies"'. Furthermore, there is an attempt to formulate a systematic comparison of the observed peculiarities across cases. It was argued in Chapter One that actors translate or interpret new ideas and use them alongside existing systems and processes (see for example Scarbrough and Corbett, 1992). Such sense-making processes can be more thoroughly investigated by immersing oneself in the daily activities of the research participants, made possible by participant observation. Douglas (1976 in Gill and Johnson, 1991, p. 109) argues that 'participant observation can enable the researcher to penetrate various complex form of "misinformation, fronts, evasions and lies" that are considered endemic in most social settings.' This method allows one to be sensitive to the context-dependent, specific and tacit nature of diffused work systems. Action-oriented knowledge based on organizational routines cannot be discerned entirely through interviews. Interviews can provide only an incomplete account of the dynamic interplay of archetypes and negotiated patterns of interaction between different groups of social actors. This research is not only concerned with discrete taxonomies, such as structural elements, of work systems diffusion. It also aims to examine the social relations and processes in which activities are embodied (Clark and Newell, 1993).

The research focuses on participants' perceptions of continuous improvement activities and related changes in work practices and structures. The challenge here is to understand and interpret complex forms of social activity, which are defined by the actors themselves in terms of their own subjective meanings. The internal logic of participants' meaning cannot be addressed by positivist methods borrowed from the natural sciences. In order to explore the experience of the workers under the 'Japanese' model, one needs to live, act and think the specific meaning and relevance structure of the social agents (see Delbridge, 1998). However, in the present research, this is not carried to the extreme of being fully immersed in the activities of a given firm and, hence, the researcher can stand back and relate the variables under observation. One week's factory work experience in two of the UK sites provided the opportunity to elicit adopters' perspective and examine practice (see Altheide and Johnson, 1998).

Three qualitative case studies were conducted to attain a rigorous comparison of the diffusion process. It was felt that a comparison of two subsidiary firms alone would not have provided the diversity necessary in the investigation of the likely influences on the internalization of alternative work systems. Three cases could yield more data than two cases where flow and configuration of events and reactions influencing a particular degree of internalization of work systems would become clear. A replication study (Yin, 1994) was necessary whereby 'successive cases [could be] examined to see whether the new pattern matche[d] the one found earlier' (Huberman and Miles, 1998, p. 195). Each case was selected to produce contrasting results but for predictable reasons to attain a 'theoretical replication' (see Yin, 1994). According to Yin at least four cases need to be designed to pursue two different patterns of theoretical replication. There was not a case that was similar to the Rover–Honda collaboration in the UK automotive sector, thus a fourth comparable site could not be added to the sample. The Rover–Honda collaboration was a complex alliance in the sense that R&D, manufacturing, development and sourcing of parts were joint. The marketing and sales were the only separate areas (see Faulkner, 1995).

The aim was to strike a balance between collecting data that allowed for a rigorous analysis and avoiding data overload in the field, 'leading to the analysts thus missing important information, overweighing some findings, skewing the analysis' (Huberman and Miles, 1998, p. 198).

The interview type and protocol

Data were mainly gathered through interviews. The research minimized the respondent bias by triangulating data through participant observation and document analysis. This, as will be outlined in Section Three, was a means of establishing validity in the context of reflective accounting. Denzin and Lincoln (1998, p. 278) refer to this process as 'analytic realism'. In Hammersley's (1992, p. 69) terms, analytic realism aims to 'represent accurately those features of the phenomena that it is intended to describe, explain or theorize'.

At the two UK subsidiary firms, part of the information drew on work experience over a week in June and July 1999. Further information came from interviews with Japanese advisors, directors, UK team leaders, operators and managers across personnel and training, sales and marketing, product engineering, design and quality, and finance between August 1998 and January 2000. In addition, information was obtained through interviews with the Japanese managers in product development, general affairs, quality assurance, corporate finance, engineering and corporate planning and control departments at the parent companies and factory tours in Japan in April 2000 (see Appendix II for a list of interviewees at both subsidiary firms). The research questions addressed the nature of the relationship, and the division of responsibility between the Japanese MNC and the subsidiary. They also considered the means of diffusion, characteristics that facilitated and inhibited the diffusion process, perceived cultural and managerial differences between the two companies and learning opportunities available to the parent and subsidiary companies. Interviews from multiple functions were drawn for a representative account of the ways in which knowledge-driven work systems were sustained in the firms. The aim of the inquiry was to reveal the different truths and realities held by different individuals across sections within a firm as well as groups across nations (see Stringer, 1996). Participant observation at Teniki UK and Nissera UK was limited to a week owing to the change in the employees' work schedule.[4] Thus, interviews with factory personnel and managers were necessary to attain a complete picture of the social patterns in the factory. Interviews were also necessary for background information on the factory structure and work relations at the time of the company's foundation, for these patterns, given their occurrence in the past, could not be experienced in person.

At the technical collaboration site, the perceptions of research participants on the past collaborative project were gathered through interviews and document analysis. Interviews at Rover were conducted between January 1999 and September 1999 with 23 employees, including senior managers across design, purchasing and manufacturing. Discussions focused on how the R8/YY project that commenced in 1985 (with a model launch in 1989), was carried out by the electrical engineers in a framework of diffused Japanese quality improvement philosophies and techniques. There was a focus on electrical engineers, as their working relations with Honda members were seen as better than those in other departments at Rover, hence characteristics that were likely to facilitate the internalization of Japanese work systems could be more easily identified. Interviews focused on the views of 18 engineers based at Rover since the time of the collaboration, who were involved at some stage in the R8/YY project. Nine of the engineers constituted the core team of the 30 electrical engineers who visited Japan and served liaison roles for six to 12 months. The nature of the research questions addressed to the subsidiary firms applied to the Rover–Honda collaboration as well. In addition, specific Honda practices that were diffused to Rover and implemented at the time of the R8/YY project, as well as the impact of mechanisms for sharing ideas on the effectiveness of the collaboration were explored. In brief, the questions focused on the knowledge-sharing dimension within the engineering project and diffusion across the two companies. The same questions were also directed to ten Honda members. Four of these were principal engineers on the R8/YY project based in Japan. One of the Honda members was the project manager on the R8/YY and another occupied a managerial position on the XX project. The remaining four were senior managers. One of the senior managers was based at Honda R&D UK, the second at Honda of the UK Manufacturing Ltd., and the remaining two at the Rover Liaison Office of Honda Motor Europe Ltd. (see Appendix II for a list of interviewees at Rover and Honda). Some of the engineers on the team (four at Rover and five at Honda) could not be interviewed, as they were no longer affiliated with the company (mainly in the case of Rover) and the electrical engineering department (in the case of Honda). In addition, there were resource constraints with regard to the three-week visit to Japan. Rover members were approached via snowball sampling with letters and fax messages sent to the recommended research participants. A similar approach was pursued at Honda. The author was recommended to a Honda member by a trustworthy British counterpart at Rover. Honda R&D in Utsunomiya and Honda Headquarters in Aoyama, Japan, were visited for interviews during March and April 2000. The engineers provided specific project-related information, whilst senior managers provided the history of the collaboration, including its industrial and economic background. In addition to formal interviews, there were informal conversations with Rover engineers that allowed interpretations following interviews to be clarified and confirmed.

Rover and Honda employees were cooperative and relatively open about their experiences during the R8/YY joint work. It was a project carried out in the past and the commercial sensitivity of the information provided was no longer an issue. As the research was a retrospective study of the diffusion of Honda practices to the UK partner, Rover members could reflect more rationally upon their joint work by presenting both their negative and positive experiences. During discussions, participants were engaged in the process of reflecting on their experiences rather than living them. This enabled them to better articulate their experiences and perceptions. A retrospective study could reduce the likely occurrence of an attribution bias, where a negative occurrence is attributed to an external cause rather than an internal interpretation (that is something within the personal control of the respondent) (McKenna, 1994). Respondents at Rover could hold their group members or company responsible for mistakes or managerial deficiencies over the course of their collaboration with Honda.[5] The author was sensitive to the possibility that members could over-rationalize their experiences. Efforts were made to minimize such drawbacks.

The interviews in the sampled firms were open-ended and semi-structured, and addressed the incorporation of Japanese continuous improvement techniques (operationalized as team-based work or change in authority relations) and philosophies (operationalized as the values of a team ethos and personal/cultural control) into the UK adopter firms. Information was sought on the meaning for individuals of events, relationships, social structures, roles and norms (see Appendix III for a list of interview questions). Data on the degree of internalization were obtained from field observations and on-the-job discussions with the operators. The quotes are based on verbatim transcripts.

Protocols (Yin, 1994) incorporating schedules of company visits and members to be interviewed were developed. The majority of the interviews were taped and transcribed.[6] Wherever possible, a confirmation of the contents of the transcriptions was sought. The resulting data were processed into reports and sent to gatekeepers at each company for feedback.

The research methods employed in the three firms are detailed in Table 3.2.

The research questions were translated into Japanese and presented to each participant interviewed in Japan together with the English version for a clearer understanding of the concepts presented. The Japanese version of the questions was sent to the participants based in Japan in advance of the author's visit to the Japanese parent and partner firms. Both the English and the Japanese versions of the interview questions were developed on the basis of the levels and concepts presented in the analytic framework (see Chapter One), and deduced from the research questions (see Introduction). The list of interview questions was divided into three sections. The first section

Table 3.2   *Data collection at Teniki UK, Nissera UK and the*
              Rover–Honda collaboration

Activity	Teniki UK	Nissera UK	Rover–Honda
Document analysis	Company reports, local development agency reports	Company reports, local development agency reports	DTI reports, journal and newspaper articles, books, internal reports
Interviews in the UK	18 (Aug 1998– Jan 2000)	14 (Apr–Sept 1999)	25 (Jan–Sept 1999)
Interviews in Japan	2 (April 2000)	6 (April 2000)	8 (March–April 2000)
Total number of interviews	*20*	*20*	*33*
Participant observation (in the UK)	1 week as operator in car component assembly (July 1999)	1 week as operator in car component assembly (June 1999)	—
Factory tours in Japan	Saitama plant, car component assembly, blow moulding and press shops (April 2000)	Car component production and assembly, R&D centre (April 2000)	[Tour of Rover's Longbridge plant (June 1999)]

Source: Data collected between 1998 and 2000

aimed to capture the institutional elements that could have an impact on the implementation and internalization of work systems at the adopter firms. In the second section, there was a focus on organizational characteristics, such as structural and cultural elements, that could influence the diffusion process. The questions in this section were preceded by a historical discussion of the establishment of the organization (when and by whom, in other words which key actors were involved in the process of establishment). The range of products manufactured, customers served and size (in terms of the number of employees) of the company, provided by the gatekeepers in each firm, were also considered. In addition, questions about employee attitudes towards alternative work systems at the factory and the engineering project level were addressed. Participants were asked for their perceptions of the method of diffusion, and performance implications of and worker response to alternative work systems.

2. DATA ANALYSIS

The analysis of data is based on Djelic's (1998 based on John Stuart Mill's two-sided comparative method) two-step comparative historical analysis. It combines detailed case studies that ensure 'historical and contextual singularities are not being disregarded' with systematic comparison that 'allows for a significant theoretical leverage and represents a powerful tool, thus making generalization possible' (Djelic, 1998, p. 14). In-depth case studies highlighted the conditions underlying a given degree of internalization of Japanese work systems. Interview transcriptions and observation notes were scanned to generate a list of tentative sub-themes within the main themes of structural, cultural, control-related and technological work systems identified in the literature as having an impact on employee perceptions. Iterative loops of adding and amending sub-themes led to those that were identified as the most important in explaining the diffusion process.

Sub-themes that were not comparable across the three companies or were only mentioned by a single respondent were not included in the analysis. For example, the production manager at Nissera UK (30 July 1999) indicated a lack of interest in suggestion schemes on the part of workers: 'We have launched it [the suggestion scheme] twice. People are just not motivated.' This particular component of a continuous improvement scheme was not diffused to Teniki UK, hence was excluded from the findings. The answers to more pertinent questions, such as barriers to the diffusion of work systems, focused on a communication barrier between the Japanese and the British. As other respondents acknowledged a communication barrier, theoretical saturation was reached on this issue and the 'level of communication' was included as one of the sub-themes in the analysis.

A 'method of difference' was adopted for comparing cases with different degrees of internalization. 'Instead of comparing different instances of a phenomenon, to discover in what they agree, this method compares an instance of its occurrence with an instance of its non-occurrence, to discover in what they differ' (Mill, 1974, p. 391). By comparing divergent cases, the author was able to identify, in Djelic's term, 'bundles of conditions' that accounted for variations in outcomes. This approach reflects Eisenhardt's (1989) coupling of within-case data analysis with cross-case patterns for a more sophisticated understanding, or Boyatzis' (1998) identification of themes within samples and their comparison across subsamples. It is basically a method of elimination based on 'the successive exclusion of the various circumstance which are found to accompany a phenomenon in a given instance, in order to ascertain what are those among them which can be absent consistently with the existence of the phenomenon' (Mill, 1974, p. 392). The 'method of difference' is founded on the principle that whatever cannot be eliminated is connected with the phenomenon under investigation.

3.   RELIABILITY AND VALIDITY CONCERNS

Qualitative case studies, including participant observation, which involves the immersion of the researcher into the social setting under study, can be regarded by those with a positivist approach to methodology as highly sub-jective (see for example Schatzman and Strauss, 1973). For example, the researcher may be seen as impacting on the social setting, or forced to rely on his/her own perceptions. Depending on the circumstance, representations need to be given credence or legitimated through cross-checking. The research reported here employs multiple data collection as a means of minimizing inaccurate interpretations. Multiple cases, multiple informants within each case and across nations (that is, interviews with both British and Japanese members), and more than one data gathering method are used to strengthen the study's usefulness for other settings (see Marshall and Rossman, 1995).

This study counter-challenges what the traditional canons perceive as a weakness – low external validity – in qualitative research by explicating the theoretical parameters of the study. It presents how data collection and analysis were guided by concepts. Trouble was taken to participate in the factory activities of workers, taking into account the opinions and actions of the people with whom the researcher interacted. Nonetheless, as the researcher was part of the social world that was being studied and had intrinsic values and beliefs from which she could not wholly detach herself, absolute neutrality or true objectivity was impossible to achieve. Under this circumstance, the challenge for the researcher was to be conscious of any factors that could render the study 'unintelligible, unrepresentative, or irrel-evant' (Delbridge, 1998, p. 18). In the given study, the impact of the researcher's presence on the findings was minimized by forming relation-ships with the members in social settings.

Measures were taken to ensure that quality aspects, including reliability, construct validity, internal validity and external validity were incorporated into the study.[7] There was still a need to organize and interpret observations in qualitative research in a systematic way.

Reliability

The reliability of the research results was enhanced by making explicit the procedures that had been followed for data collection. These procedures included matters of interview protocol, tape-recordings of interviews and the feedback on transcriptions from the participants, as well as building and sustaining relationships in the field.[8] Also of importance was the collecting of secondary information,[9] such as journal and newspaper articles, Department of Trade and Industry publications, publications on the Rover–Honda collaboration and company reports.

Construct Validity

Due to the nature of the kind of information sought, concerned as it was with the meaning for individuals of events, relationships, social structures, roles and norms, there was no easy means of checking validity. If true meaning is what the credible members say it is, it is necessary to decide how many participants one should interview in order to have a clear picture of the social patterns in a given organization. A valid picture of the researched phenomenon is attained here through theoretical saturation. This is defined by Glaser and Strauss (1967) as an instance when a researcher interviews members of a specific group about the meaning of some aspect of reality and the same responses, themes, concerns and feelings come up again and again. When 'no additional data [can be] found whereby the sociologist can develop properties of the category', theoretical saturation has been reached on this issue for this group (ibid., p. 61). In addition, this study adopts a multilevel approach. It investigates knowledge-driven work systems diffusion at the institutional and organizational levels, which is useful in saturating categories of incidents. It is argued that a multilevel approach is necessary to provide a representative account of a complex organizational phenomenon as that of cross-national diffusion of work systems (see Kostova, 1999).

Initial concepts and frameworks were tested through preliminary interviews, while research sites were being explored. This testing was carried out at an early stage in the research process. Questions were semi-structured, so as to provide for consistency across the cases in the message conveyed to the participants. The semi-structured questioning also provided the opportunity to probe issues deeper to obtain an in-depth understanding of the key characteristics that were likely to shape the process of internalizing Japanese work systems. This questioning provided the researcher with the flexibility to track key issues as they emerged. In addition, participant observation made it possible to capture, understand and analyse social relations and processes. It allowed the researcher to examine the main activities of the working day and in particular how participants '[took] recourse to context-linked typifications in order to make sense of their activities' (Hassard, 1993, p. 98). It was necessary to learn the informal rules that were being followed and the way these were interpreted.

Multiple sources of confirmation were necessary to clarify meaning and to verify the repeatability of an interpretation (see Raymond, 1996). Data were drawn from interviews, participant observation and document analysis. Moreover, within the case companies, interview data from a particular work group were checked against responses from another group. For example, factory workers' accounts in two of the cases were triangulated with the team leaders' and managers' accounts. Similarly, British and Japanese participants' accounts were cross-checked against each other. This helped minimize possible translation errors.

Individual case findings were presented in various conferences for cross-checking the use of research concepts. This was also a check for coherence of arguments. In other words, there was a check to ascertain whether the conclusions followed from the premises, and correspondence. Interpretations had to be written or staged as a presentation that required direct response from an audience.

Interview data were also cross-checked with research participants. Company reports circulated for feedback served to validate research results. There were several employees with whom the researcher interacted regularly and to whom she was able to go back to whenever there was a need for elaboration and clarification.

Internal Validity

To arrive at insights into the relationship between institutional variation and work systems diffusion, Yin's (1994) principle of pattern-matching was employed. The case studies revealed how and why a particular degree of internalization of Japanese work systems occurred. There was an intensive search for patterns in key characteristics that explained a given level of internalization. After analysing the historical constituents of each case, events of each company were compared and contrasted to reveal similarities and differences. These results were then compared with the research questions about the influence of institutional and organizational elements on the diffusion of Japanese knowledge-driven work systems. The two-step comparative historical analysis promoted the internal validity of the research by minimizing the possibility of misinterpretations caused by the researcher's selective perception.

External Validity

The domain to which findings could be generalized was the historical neo-institutional framework in an analytic rather than statistical form. As the research aim was to explain the complexity of social exchange in a factory setting and on a collaborative project to highlight the key concepts constituting the diffusion process, the statistical generalizability of findings to other settings was not of concern in this study. However, it was possible to arrive at empirical pointers for the future. A future step would be to investigate conceptually similar but apparently contrasting situations (see Bechhofer and Paterson, 2000).

This research focused on the cognitive systems and normative patterns that outlined the expected mode of social relationships in a factory and joint project setting. Other research strategies, such as surveys and archival analysis, were considered as constrained in their potential to tap into the 'mental models in which human beings create working models of the world by making and manipulating analogies in their minds' (Nonaka and Takeuchi, 1995, p. 60). In this context, it becomes more meaningful to rephrase the question of whether case studies are generalizable to a form that reads as follows: 'In what sense is a case study representative?' Reflecting upon the matter, one could draw patterns of behaviour in a particular group of organizations. For example, firms located on greenfield sites may reflect levels of internalization that are different from those located on brownfield sites. The case companies illuminated and developed the analytic framework presented in Chapter One and, hence, were treated in some sense as representative.

4. SUMMARY

The research design is based on a comparative analysis of firms operating in similar industries with similar diffused work systems, but on different sites and under different forms of ownership. The focus of the research is more on the processual than structural aspects of the diffusion process. In this way, limits to comparing firms of different structural parameters are reduced.

Data were collected between 1998 and 2000 at two UK subsidiary firms, Japanese parent companies, and an Anglo-Japanese technical collaboration, with interviews conducted at both partner firms. The selection of firms included brownfield and greenfield subsidiary firms and a technical collaboration 'committed' to continuous improvement activities in the automotive manufacturing sector. Criteria considered in the selection of firms included site, sector, form of ownership, and the nature of diffused work systems, in other words, efforts to achieve continuous improvement in quality and reliability.

Data relating to employee and managerial perceptions of the way in which Japanese knowledge-driven work systems were diffused to adopter firms and the characteristics that had an impact on their implementation and internalization were gathered via semi-structured interviews with the following groups of people: Japanese advisors, British and Japanese directors, senior managers, and British team leaders and operators. Participant observation in factory settings was also of importance in securing such data. Additional data were collected from secondary sources including company reports, DTI reports, journal and newspaper articles, books and local council reports. Interviews were based on a pre-defined schedule and a list of questions (that is, an interview protocol) aimed at capturing institutional and organizational influences. All interviews, with the exception of the 12 with British employees and those with Japanese members, were recorded, transcribed and fed back to the gatekeepers.

The data analysis took the form of a two-step comparative historical analysis. Interview transcriptions and observation notes were scanned for tentative sub-themes, and key sub-themes were selected upon iterative loops of adding and amending. The systematic comparison of data, based on a 'method of difference', allowed the author to highlight the key influences on a given outcome.

A range of methods and techniques for qualitative research was used to enhance the reliability and validity of the results. Reliability was enhanced through explicating methods used in data collection, such as tape-recordings of interviews and feedback from participants. Construct validity was promoted through preliminary interviews, triangulation of data and feedback from academics at conferences. Internal validity was enhanced through pattern-matching of key explanatory characteristics across the three cases. External validity was promoted through analytic generalization, where research findings were fed back to the analytic framework adopted earlier.

NOTES

1. There were no confidentiality concerns in the Rover–Honda case, as the research focused on a past project and the collaboration came to an end in 1994.
2. At the Rover–Honda collaboration site, this period covers 1978 to 1989, in other words the year of establishment to the completion of the R8/YY project.
3. 'Knowledge transfer' is used intentionally here to reflect the linearity assumed in the diffusion of knowledge.
4. The number of working days was reduced from five to four days due to a drop in the sales volume of major customers. This was a measure taken to avoid lay-offs.
5. The same did not necessarily apply to Honda members. This might have been due to the strong implications that the norm of losing face has in the Japanese culture. At the same time, interviews with Honda engineers were held in the presence of two senior Honda members, one of whom had recently retired. The retired member acted as a translator, at times, during the interviews.
6. Seven Rover, one Nissera UK and four Teniki UK interviews with British respondents

were not taped, as the conditions under which the interviews were conducted were not suitable for recording. There were very few instances where the researcher felt that the tape recorder led to withholding of data by the participants. Notes were taken in the case of interviews with Japanese participants. Given the language difficulty and the specific trust-building mechanism in Japanese society (where heavy emphasis is placed on goodwill trust that forms over time), note-taking rather than tape-recording was necessary. Moreover, note-taking allowed Japanese respondents to demonstrate the issue at hand by sketching it on paper.

7. Although the terms 'validity' and 'reliability' are borrowed from positivist natural sciences to test for the coherence of the study (particularly given the fact that a systematic comparison is performed), they do not imply a simple causality between the phenomena under investigation. There is an attempt to capture the complexity of understanding, in addition to providing an explanation of why things are how they are. In other words, the research adopts 'theoretical realism' rather than a truly naturalistic perspective.

8. This helped in attaining considerable degree of internal coherence and plausibility (see Atkinson, 1990).

9. According to Eisenhardt (1989), prior research and literature about a subject can provide a valuable source for comparative analysis and validating theory.

4. Appropriation of Japanese work systems in the UK: illustrations from the automotive industry

Teniki UK, Nissera UK and Rover faced similar environmental pressures to be innovative and competitive. They aimed to enhance manufacturing skills and the quality and productivity of their output by adopting lean manufacturing systems and continuous improvement. However, conscious efforts to institutionalize meanings, values and norms at these sites were not very effective in changing organizational behaviour. Although the major practices diffused were similar in all three companies, the degree to which they were infused with value and accepted in each site differed. The degree of implementation and internalization of work systems was significantly higher at Nissera UK and the Rover–Honda collaboration than at Teniki UK.

1. NATURE OF DIFFUSED WORK SYSTEMS

Organizational Structure: the Shift to Team Structure

There was a shift in work organization at all three sites towards a flatter team structure. The pattern of authority relations at the two subsidiaries was changed from one based on superintendents, supervisors and hourly paid workers to one built around team leaders, team coaches and hourly paid workers arranged in a production cell layout rather than assembly lines.

At Teniki UK, the transition to a team structure was based on the objectives of reducing costs and supervisor autonomy and breaking 'them and us' clusters in the company.

> We had less number of supervisors, hence it was a cost-saving measure in that way. We had a lot who did not understand the difference between a team coach and a supervisor. With the new structure, there is a lot more concentration on the training side. Team coaches have more man-management and planning responsibilities. All team coaches are trained to train people. The benefits will take some time to reap. (British personnel and training assistant, 29 July 1999)

Nissera UK's management of work teams on the shop floor in 1997 was seen as essential due to the plunge in profits in 1995 and 1996. According to the General Affairs Department of Nissera (e-mail sent on 20 October 2000):

> From 1993 to 1996, sales rose satisfactorily but profits were getting worse. Profits in 1995 and 1996 fell sharply because of the strong Yen and the failure to local- ize [value-added car component] assembly. After that year, 1998 and 1999 marked the best sales in the past due to support from Nissera[1] and the reduction in the value of the Yen. [See Appendix IV for the sales and profit trends between 1993 and 1999.]

At Rover, there was a shift from functional authority relations to a project-based structure in 1985. Formerly, Rover allocated resources to different functions, with individuals working on a number of projects. A core expertise could not be sustained within such a structure. By contrast, within a project-based structure, engineers who were assigned to project teams could consult a central pool of expertise on technical difficulties.

At Teniki UK, the segregation between management and workers led to difficulties in instilling high levels of commitment among operators. Team-working was better received by operators at Nissera UK, where the shift to a team structure was associated with the build-up of skills imparted by Japanese expatriates in the early years after the company's establishment. However, the fluid job descriptions evident in the Japanese parent compa- nies were not widely observed in the UK subsidiaries. Operators perceived team leaders as above the work group, rather than as members of the team. Team leaders and assistants at Nissera UK had clearly defined responsibil- ities and their positions were treated as managerial ones. This is reflected in the production manager's (30 July 1999) claim that 'team leaders do not do the work. As long as they make sure the system is in, what comes out is efficiency, cost and quality.'

At Rover, the project-based structure adopted with R8/YY was seen as promoting a team effort to solve problems quickly and deliver projects on time.

> There is something uniting everyone and that is the delivery date. You feel more exposed to the pressures of working for an engineering firm. Whereas in a functionally-based organisation, people are more interested in getting more focused on becoming an expert on their project. There is less of a focus on the actual delivery of a project and more on a delivery of their part. There is less immediate pressure to hit that delivery date and there is a problem of getting people to work together. (principal electrical engineer K at Rover, 2 June 1999)

Nevertheless, from Honda's perspective, the implementation of the project-based structure at Rover was not effectively carried out. Functional

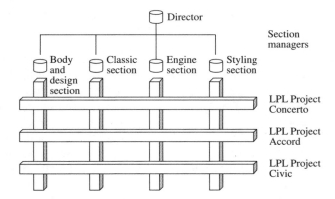

Note: LPL: Large Project Leader

Source: Interview with the Japanese executive vice-president of Honda R&D Europe, 29 March 2000

Figure 4.1 Organizational structure of Rover as perceived by Honda

managers continued to have more control than project managers (see Figure 4.1). The section managers preferred to avoid risk, whilst large project leaders wanted to take risks in order to develop a competitive, innovative product. Honda continued to uphold a project-based structure.

> We always have a weekly meeting with every project leader. Rover had a problem, because its body engineers were in Cowley, interior engineers in Canley and other engineers in Longbridge. They tried to gather and established Gaydon [where the design centre is]. (Japanese executive vice-president of Honda R&D Europe, 29 March 2000)

While communication then improved, the timing of the build phases still could not match that of Honda:

> We agreed on a schedule. Rover could not understand this schedule, could not understand how to manage or carry out their own job. Honda sets up a project manager to manage the timing. They control the progress of the team. They also receive the services of a support function. (Japanese executive vice-president of Honda R&D Europe, 29 March 2000)

Organizational Culture: Commitment to Quality Improvement Schemes

Teniki UK, Nissera UK and Rover all had difficulty in securing the commitment of all parties to the parent companies' continuous improvement schemes, such as quality circles, discipline in the workplace and the '5C' housekeeping principles (classifying, clarifying, cleanliness, clean-up and custom).

Operators and those enforcing the system at Teniki UK did not subscribe to the Japanese belief that good housekeeping improves work habits and the quality of facilities. For instance, 'people do not read the quality audits. They just put a check. Somebody at the end of the day should look at the sheets' (senior operator at Teniki UK). Older operators at Teniki UK worked according to their own rules and enjoyed the freedom created by weak control in the factory. They manhandled machines when they did not work properly, ate and drank in their cells and failed to fill in production timesheets on an hourly basis: 'I do it at the end of the day and take an average. It looks better that way.' Production pressures led to the manipulation of scrap-rate figures. An assembler commented: 'Quality Assurance is called over when there is a supplier-related problem. If there is a pressure to get the order out, then they will pass the item that I would normally scrap.' (However, a team coach at Teniki UK commented that the Japanese also manipulated their scrap rates). The Teniki UK operations manager summarized the situation in the plant as follows:

> The biggest thing, which we have not been successful in, I suppose, is the Kaizen, small group activity work. We all know the benefits of doing that but again, the managers and engineers can actually carry on these activities, but unless the people on the shop floor buy into them and understand them and want to be part of them, it is not sustainable. You can create Kaizen activity, get [the desired] result and potentially walk away. And if the people do not buy into it and understand why they are doing it, it is wasted. Because we have not cascaded the information down and have not got the skills bottom up to top, we cannot achieve this sustainable continuous improvement within the plant. (British operations manager, 18 January 2000)

The previous ownership focused on teaching skills that were related to an operator's immediate task rather than the overall production process. Although job training under current management was typically provided internally and included consultation with staff, the training and development plan had not instilled a continuous improvement culture at Teniki UK.

> I believe, people [direct labour] understand that they need to cut costs in the business. However, the adoption of the approaches and the ownership of correcting the problems, they do not do. That again is partly through training and the pressure on the business, not being able to release them to train because the first thing we need to do is keep our customer happy. We had a massive delivery problem when I joined. We are now sort of 99.9 per cent day in day out. Now that is stabilized, we can go back to people. (British operations manager, 18 January 2000)

Similarly, operators at Nissera UK failed to internalize continuous improvement schemes, owing to the way local management administered Kaizen initiatives:

> We were forced to go on this course [on quality circles]. They called it 'family circle'. It is a big joke. Everything is a joke. It could be better if they were straighter with us. As long as we are concerned, they have deceived us. They will start with something and if it does not suit them, they will change it. (assembler at Nissera UK)

Some of the operators saw 5Cs as 'basically cleanliness, [it] is more cosmetic than anything else' (team leader at Nissera UK, 14 June 1999). The author's own work experience in one of the production cells showed inconsistency in the application of quality standards. The researcher was shown how to conduct a quality control check on component assembly. This involved checking the strength of screw tightening and loosening, and plotting the observed measure on a quality control chart. The assembler who was demonstrating the process recorded the measure as falling within the quality tolerance levels although the figure was clearly outside the limits. The low sense of responsibility for quality control processes could also be observed in the 'parts testing' phase of the assembly process. Tests normally took seven minutes to complete. However, operators found this too long and halted the process after two or three minutes. Furthermore, forms that were filled in on rejects and reworks were frequently recorded as 'other supplier's fault' rather than 'self responsibility' or 'machine fault'.

> We supply many products to [our biggest customer]. We know that the 100 components from Nissera will be good. We cannot be so sure at Nissera UK [even though] the control system is not so different from Nissera. For instance, the process quality control chart is the same as that at Nissera. Over the past two years we have tended to go back to Japanese parts. Every single part needs to meet quality standards. In the UK, the attitude is, out of a million, surely there can be few defects. There is a wider tolerance level in a European supplier context. This is not the case in Japan. Customers, unlike in the UK, expect zero defects in Japan. (Japanese quality director at Nissera UK, 13 September 1999)

In the early years of the Rover–Honda collaboration, there seemed to be more emphasis on results than on processes. Underlying philosophies were learnt over time as more projects of a collaborative nature were carried out. The commitment to quality improvement schemes in car development was low until 1985. With the initiation of the R8/YY project, there was an improvement in the level of commitment to such schemes. The dedication was even higher on subsequent projects, particularly with the launch of the Rover 200 model in 1989.

For example, Honda practices such as the *gebba-kai* process (that is, quality circles adopted by engineers to solve problems at the end of each build phase) and formalized build phases were approximated and never fully realized. The *gebba-kai* process basically consisted of one or two days set aside in a project after a build sequence to iron out problems, to do, for example, with parts not fitting properly or with misunderstandings between engineering and manufacturing. Suppliers were also invited to these meetings when problems could not be resolved internally. Rover engineers were able to observe the *gebba-kai* process during their six to 12 months' joint engineering work with Honda engineers in Japan.

While *gebba-kai* was seen as valuable by Rover (in the words of a team leader, 'they forced us to use it but since they have left we have still used it'), implementation differed from Honda practice. Although the intention was to have an internal and an external *gebba-kai* as at Honda, Rover had 'changed it a little for the worst' (British senior manager in manufacturing integration), with fewer days devoted to it and fewer people attending problem-resolution sessions. The *gebba-kai* meetings failed to see things through to decisions. According to a Rover design and development engineer (23 June 1999):

> The aim is to always arrive at a decision. I think if we followed it [*gebba-kai*] literally and the way some of the Honda engineers worked, then yes, we would always arrive at a decision because they would not leave without a decision.

Rover's build phases were formalized to match Honda's evolutionary process in car development.

> Learning from Honda was that you must go through a process of evolution and all the components that fit into the vehicle must be off-tool and off-process. One of the requirements that Honda laid down was that the more you practised, the better the product. (British principal systems engineer on Rover 800, G, 10 May 1999).

However, Honda's methodical steps in delivering components contrasted with Rover's relatively ad hoc approach. Processes had been tested before, hence there were clear reasons as to why Honda engineers strictly abided by them. By contrast, Rover engineers tended to apply processes as they saw fit. 'I think we tend to look for compromise and modify as appropriate or we feel we have to because we have money constraints' (principal systems engineer on Rover 800, G, 10 May 1999). Honda members were perceived by Rover engineers as following instructions to the letter: 'The Japanese always comply with their orders. We will comply if the orders suit us' (ibid.). By contrast, employees in the UK context would try to find an alternative method of carrying out a task rather than work to a rigid process. According to a senior manager in manufacturing integration, Rover lacked the self-discipline rigourously to prove a process, train people and introduce double checks to stabilize the system. This was observed in the way Rover raised Project Change Requests (PCRs):

> Again we might not have the discipline that they adopt in terms of the PCR changes. PCRs are supposed to be all resolved and signed off at the [*gebba-kai*] event. But not everybody turns up. Sometimes it is quite difficult to judge whether you should invite all your suppliers, because some of our suppliers come a long way. So we might not have the discipline to fully do it but we still basically adopt it. (principal electrical engineer I at Rover, 24 May 1999)

Control Mechanism: Degree of Involvement by the Japanese

Although the extent to which Japanese expatriates were involved in the day-to-day running of the business and in manpower planning differs across the three cases, the pressure exerted by the Japanese company on technical and strategic issues was considerable in the two subsidiary firms. At Teniki UK, there was high indirect involvement by Japanese management in the activities of the subsidiary. There was considerable financial pressure from the parent company, in terms of demands for rapid profitability, despite the parent's interest in developing skills at the UK operation.

> Teniki [Japanese parent company] have pressure on them to put pressure on ourselves to make the returns faster than normal. In that case, we have had to have very stringent sort of budgetary control and cutting of budgets which would affect the long-term, that is the training budgets are not as good as they should be in my belief. (British operations manager at Teniki UK, 18 January 2000)

The majority of products at Teniki UK were designed around Japanese processes.

> They still require us to put in place best practice processes such as U-shaped cells, Single Minute Exchange of Dies (SMED), assembly cells, where minimum stock levels of product are within reach, ergonomically designed. So they expect best practice. However, achieving some of the best practices is problematic. (British operations manager at Teniki UK, 18 January 2000)

The type of control exercised was impersonal and technocratic through output control and planning with clear-cut quantitative objectives at both strategic and operational levels (see Harzing, 2001).

Similarly, the parent company of Nissera UK was heavily involved in decisions on providing technology and investment finance for the subsidiary.

However, Nissera did not exert stringent budgetary control over the UK firm, at least in the first three years of operation. Instead, it exercised personal and cultural control through direct supervision and the use of expatriates:

> Sometimes we do not chase profit. Otherwise we would be money traders. We invest. Our profit is generated from the products we manufacture. We sometimes try to forget about profitability. For the first three years, we do not expect a profit. We expect a profit in the fourth, fifth year. (manager in the corporate planning and control department at Nissera, 14 April 2000)

Nissera's commitment to broad range and long-lasting effort to create the dedicated human and organizational capabilities decreased as its UK subsidiary failed to develop its own knowledge base and satisfactory results.

> First time I was in the UK, we brought know-how with documentation and information [such as quality standards, instruction manuals, QC process charts and drawings]. Japan did not send any know-how after that. Their manufacturing is old and manual, so we cannot transfer know-how. (Japanese quality assurance manager at Nissera, 13 April 2000)

As at Teniki UK, the responsibility for design rested with the parent company, and the subsidiary operated more as an assembly operation dependent on imports of manufactured inputs from Japan (see Elger and Smith, 1994).

At Rover, the pressure by local management on engineers to follow the 'Honda' way in design and development became apparent during the R8/YY project: 'As the project went on, we were more and more subtly encouraged to go the Honda way on everything. In essence, we adapted our specifications to meet theirs at the end of the day' (principal electrical engineer I at Rover, 21 June 1999). Nevertheless, as Rover was not wholly owned by Honda, Honda's exercise of control did not take the form of direct supervision as in the other two firms. At Rover, personal and cultural control was exercised more through socialization, informal communication and management training. Rover's liaison officers facilitated information flow and helped forge good working relations with the Japanese. Engineers saw it as essential to build social relations based on trust, for 'you could have a discussion and there would be lots of nodding and agreeing, and it did not mean they agreed with what you were saying' (principal electrical engineer H at Rover, 21 June 1999). The main concern was not whether information flowed back and forth, but whether the message was conveyed correctly and this depended on working relationship with Honda engineers.

As you got to know more and more of their engineers, and they got to know us, we would be designing things in the pub afterwards with Honda engineers. We would draw a design on a beer mat, pass it over to a Honda engineer. He would improve it and give it back to me. That would spark another idea in him and then we shake on that. And then the next day, he would draw it up. We used to do a lot of our work like that. (principal mechanical engineer L at Rover, 22 June 1999)

Technology Diffusion

Teniki UK, Nissera UK and Rover, in comparison with their parent/ partner companies, are not profound examples of advanced technology. While George and Levie (1984, p. 26) argue that 'the Japanese industry is not leagues "ahead" of us in terms of use of robots and automated equipment', there is evidence from the cases to suggest that the Japanese parent/partner companies are more technologically advanced than their UK affiliate firms, at least in the automotive manufacturing industry.

Teniki UK lacks design responsibility and serves more as a manufacturing facility despite an investment in 1999 in a technical centre and an extension to its factory. Neither its level of automation nor the reliability of its machinery in assembly is high. For example, the pleating line in the air element section had 100 per cent rework before part of the line was replaced by Japanese Teniki engineers in 1998. The line previously had a manual knob with which one could adjust the distance between pleats. This was replaced with rollers and metal disks for automatic separation of pleats and the scrap rate was reduced to 20 per cent.

Nissera had a much wider product range than its UK division. For instance, it was heavily involved in liquid crystal display (LCD) production and directed development of techniques for automobile products to new products such as water heaters and air conditioner remote controls. Nissera cited two reasons for the limited diffusion of technology. First, Nissera UK was not perceived as possessing the knowledge necessary to develop its own production lines. Second, 'Nissera UK has low volume and wide variety. It is difficult to introduce new technology' (Japanese production manager at Nissera, 13 April 2000).

'Nissera tries to disclose the latest information on R&D technology to the technical centre to support Nissera UK's sales activities' (Japanese electronics engineering manager at Nissera, 14 April 2000). However, Nissera UK only produced 'profitable' products rather than created advanced product technology. 'They do not need advanced technology or know-how. They cannot meet customers' advanced expectation', as 'they do not understand our product. They understand the manufacturing process, how to move the instrument, but cannot see the bigger picture, how to fit the product' (Japanese quality assurance manager at Nissera, 13 April 2000). The difficulty in the diffusion of technology was seen as associated with UK staff's lack of capability and willingness to learn.

> Even if we want to transfer [know-how], who can take it? If I want to transfer everything to the UK, they may need three times more persons. If there is a mechanical engineer, he only knows the field [of mechanical engineering]. He does not understand electronic engineering. In Japan, an engineer will know both. (Japanese quality assurance engineer at Nissera, 13 April 2000)

According to the Japanese management, Nissera UK needed greater financial resources and number of employees, larger facilities and a grasp of technique or insight into the integrated process of manufacturing. However, despite the low diffusion of technology to Nissera UK, the degree of internalization of work systems was relatively high owing to an emphasis on both structural and cultural shifts. This suggests that technology is secondary to the people-related problems of implementing Japanese work systems. It is also reflective of the Japanese emphasis on the 'soft' dimension of management (see Pascale and Athos, 1986).

Honda was seen by Rover as an 'interesting mixture of amazing craftsmanship and very high technology at the same time' (British design director, 22 June 1999). At the time of the R8/YY project, Rover was using two-dimensional drawings, whilst Honda was working with CATIA (a CAD software) for modelling. The difference in the software used did not affect the work that was carried out in the electrical department of Rover, 'because in terms of design specifications, we always dealt with paper copies' (principal electrical engineer F at Rover, 21 June 1999, see Appendix V for Honda Motor Corporation's communication network).

The white scan board served as an extremely effective tool in arriving at consensus-based decisions. Notes would be taken in Japanese and English on an electronic copy board, and handwritten copies would be distributed spontaneously to all the participants of R8/YY meetings with Honda engineers. The benefit of writing the issue on the board was that 'anybody can say "no, you have written that down wrong. You have to change it"' (principal electrical engineer H at Rover, 12 May 1999). All participants were made aware of the issues discussed and agreed upon at the meetings. The sharing of tacit knowledge required the close involvement and cooperation of the knowing subject.

> You knew exactly what was put on there, and whom it was actioned against. I think before that we were in the same meeting, everybody took notes in the way it suited them. Everybody saw things differently. With notes on whiteboards, you knew then who was actioned to do what and when they were supposed to do it.

We would all have pens in our hands and we would be sketching away . . . our communication was through sentences and paragraphs, and theirs was pictorial. (electrical group leader at Rover, 7 May 1999)

The boards were also used for documentation purposes or as a way of formalizing agreements.

If we asked a technical question such as 'is it possible that you could do this?' and the answer would come back 'very difficult, no' and that meant it was absolutely impossible . . . and making friends with them enabled contact and communication. And once you had communication you could then discuss things much better. (team leader J at Rover, 27 May 1999)

Matters subject to negotiation required personal visits. 'Emphasis on social processes is more important. Technology is there to transfer data but this is not knowledge. It is only a subset' (chief advanced power train engineer, 2 April 2000).

There was also investment in Rover's assembly lines. For example, Honda tried to modify the welding line at Longbridge during the R8/YY project. They were not able to change it, as Rover's production line was very long. 'Rover asked EG [Honda Engineering] to build the whole production line. Hence, Honda exported and installed unique equipment to build the R8/YY. Rover saw and reviewed the reconstruction plan' (Japanese project member on the XX project at Honda Motor Co. Ltd., 4 April 2000). As the R8/YY project involved a high level of common componentry and was to be manufactured at Rover's Longbridge plant, it was to Honda's benefit to invest in the UK manufacturing plant. The diffusion of technology to Rover complemented the availability of a skilful blend of people and the diffusion of tacit and explicit processes, supporting relatively high internalization of work systems by Rover engineers.

Teniki and Nissera's willingness to diffuse technology and know-how to their UK subsidiary firms was greater where there was a perceived high level of competence, an ability to develop one's knowledge base and successful performance in terms of strong financial status on the part of the subsidiary firm. At Rover, this willingness was more evident where there was perceived learning from past mistakes, similarity in goals, formalization of processes and the associated discipline in execution, and clear objectives and division of responsibility.

The Rover case clearly indicates that investment in IT could not act as a surrogate for people transfer, for Honda strongly emphasized teamwork, personal relations and trust. According to Dore (1997, p. 25), 'economic transactions in Japan are much more commonly embedded in face-to-face social relations.' Interactions are embedded in associative cultures, where people tend to utilize associations among events that may not have much of a 'logical' basis. Communication is characterized by face-to-face contact, which takes place among individuals who share a large body of information based on both historical and contextual modes (Hall, 1976 in Kedia and Bhagat, 1988, p. 566). Taggart (1998, p. 59) argues that where knowledge is tacit and difficult to codify, making it difficult to organize and transfer to dispersed contexts, 'person-to-person communication is extremely important'.

The findings at the three companies on the nature of diffused work systems are summarized in Table 4.1.

Table 4.1   Nature of diffused work systems in case study companies

Nature of work systems	Teniki UK	Nissera UK	Rover–Honda R8/YY Project
Organizational structure: participation through teams	Shift to team structure in 1999	Shift to team structure in 1997	Shift to team structure in 1985
Organizational culture: commitment to continuous improvement schemes	Low	Medium	Low until 1985 Medium until 1989 High thereafter
Control mechanism: degree of involvement by Japanese	Impersonal and technocratic through output control	Personal and cultural through direct supervision and expatriate control	Personal and cultural through socialization, informal communication and management training
Technology diffusion	Low	Low	Medium

The case study companies highlighted the role of actors in translating work systems in the diffusion of these systems. Ideas that travelled from the Japanese to the UK context could not be internalized unless they were translated. Alternative work systems were evaluated in the light of existing organizational practices and adopters' own assumptions concerning effective ways of operating, which served as a set of 'editing rules' (see Czarniawska and Sevón, 1996). The blending of the old and new practices occurred through a process of 'osmosis'. In other words, alternative practices fought their way through a 'semipermeable organizational membrane, consisting of existing power networks, organizational culture and subcultures, in order to influence the existing set of organizational visions' (Doorewaard and van Bijsterveld, 2001: 61). There was an editing or translation process where 'successes' were reformulated and assigned new meanings as they were diffused. Rules of 'social control, conformism and traditionalism' directed the translation process (see Sahlin-Andersson, 1996). Such a process is eminent even in architectural structures. The ingenious Spanish architect Gaudi's translation of nature into world-renowned architectural structures is an outstanding example. Gaudi believed that 'nature does not produce anything that is monochrome or uniform in colour: neither in vegetation nor in geology, nor in topography nor in the animal kingdom' (extract from Gaudi's diary in Cirlot, 2001, p. 21). The colours used in his polychrome often remind one more of the underwater flora and fauna than of the elements that can normally be seen in nature. Gaudi entered the world of 'natural morphology' by not copying it but transforming and integrating it into an architectural or structural-ornamental factor.

Historical neo-institutionalism offers no amplification on how institutional forces interact with actors' social responses. In line with 'new institutionalism' as presented by DiMaggio and Powell (1991), the emphasis is on rule development or institutionalization rather than the issue of change and the role of the actor. Change is permitted only by mistake. However, as Czarniawska and Sevón (1996, pp. 4–5) argue, 'people do manage to convince each other – to change their opinions, beliefs and ways of acting – and not only by mistake.'

As is revealed by the case studies, the internalization of work systems can be 'blocked or facilitated by the nature of cultural infrastructure and the role of human agencies' (Loveridge, 1987, p. 193). Continuous improvement schemes were subjected to UK operators' interpretation upon their diffusion to a new setting. Their utilization or development required the active involvement of those workers who possessed it. The reconceptualization of knowledge took the form of a dynamic interaction among episodes of external acquisition of knowledge, its use by firms and the commitment by firms to the extent that the acquired knowledge assumed taken-for-granted nature, or the attachment of a symbolic meaning and value by adopters to the practice as have the employees from the home country. Learning at Teniki UK, Nissera UK and Rover was shaped by the 'inherited' factors within the specific social structures. For example, the implementation of *gebba-kai* problem-solving sessions pointed to a translation process whereby 'external knowledge/artefacts/methods [were] "fused" with internal knowledge/ procedures/systems' (Hislop et al., 1998: 430).

2.   EXPLAINING THE PATTERNS OF IMPLEMENTATION AND INTERNALIZATION

The National Institutional Context

The case study findings show that the diffusability of work systems from a highly coordinated national business system, such as Japan's, to a compartmentalized one, such as the UK's, is hindered by conflicting institutional legacies and the variation in emphasis on tacit and explicit work systems between Japan and the UK.

As the cases indicate, there is a tendency for UK management to show interest in the diffusion of structure as opposed to the complex set of meanings attached to work systems. It is questionable to what degree local management understood the importance of intangible elements in continuous improvement schemes. The UK subsidiaries seemed to have a limited ability to generate 'organizational cultures involving high levels of worker commitment and flexibility' (Warner, 1994: 510) to underpin team-based organizational structures. For example, significant differences existed in the translation of a team structure to the British context.

This seems partly to reflect deep differences in national-institutional arrangements between Britain and Japan. There is a disjunction between the demands of a system that is strongly embedded in a network of mutual obligations and commitment, and those of a system that discourages cooperation between business partners. The ability of team leaders in the two subsidiary firms and the project leaders at Rover to maintain good communications within and across teams, and to motivate operators and engineers to engage in continuous improvement activities, was in part influenced by the institutional variation in worker commitment and flexibility between Japan and the UK. Unlike in Japan, a minimum involvement philosophy and low worker discretion have been the tradition in the UK (Dore, 1973). This is exemplified by the brownfield site in the study. 'In Japan, employees are grateful for being given a project to do. However, in the UK, there is demarcation, unionization. Employees will ask "why ask me to do the project?"' (personnel and training manager at Teniki UK, 15 February 1999). The resistance, especially among older Teniki UK operators, to alternative work systems was seen as deriving partly from the preference for traditional British work organization based on craft demarcations and union activity. Thus a senior assembler perceived problems in the diffusion of 5C housekeeping principles as resulting from different institutional processes in Japan and the UK: 'It [housekeeping] is ingrained in Japan. It goes back a long way. The European, Continental approach is different. Production, sweeping and paperwork represent three separate jobs.' In other words, production was carried out by the operator, sweeping by the apprentice and paperwork by the supervisor.

However, the variation in outcomes among the three case study firms implies that national-institutional differences cannot provide a full explanation of patterns of work systems diffusion. Key features of the local institutional contexts, such as local labour market conditions, and of organizational contexts, including company characteristics, also explain the varying degree to which alternative work systems are internalized.

The Local Institutional Context

The degree of implementation and internalization of Japanese knowledge-driven work systems differed across the three companies investigated on the basis of the location area and site of the companies, as well as the associated skills base of the workforce in the given regions. The location of Teniki UK on a brownfield site in a centre for tourism and the associated low skills base in manufacturing contrasted sharply with Nissera UK's location on a greenfield site in a centre for manufacturing with a high skills base in manufacturing. Teniki UK's local institutional setting also contrasted with the Rover–Honda collaboration's local institutional context. For example, Rover had a higher skills base than Teniki UK in the area in which it was located.

Teniki UK had been owned by a British firm before being acquired by a Japanese car component manufacturer, Teniki (a pseudonym), in 1996. The British firm had initially formed a joint venture with Teniki with the aim of gaining capacity to supply the European market. This prompted the development of a technical centre to develop car components capable of meeting relatively tight European standards on vehicle noise emissions. Teniki UK was located in a region where a large proportion of the labour force (nearly 40 per cent in 1997) was employed in the public sector. The region had low dependence on the manufacturing sector. Since 1991, 12 per cent of the working population had been employed in manufacturing (based on the 1998 figures released by the Economic Development and Tourism Unit in the region). Although statistics relating to social class by occupation in 1991 indicated that the highest percentage (18 per cent) of the population was economically active in the managerial and technical group, this skills base was concentrated in the financial services sector.

The weak manufacturing base had meant lower inward investment in the area. The US had the highest percentage of investment (40 per cent) in the area, mainly in the electronics sector. Japan, Germany and France ranked second (eight per cent).

As regards the level of industrial dispute in the South West of England, it was much lower than the industrial average in the UK over a period of 1991 to 1998, with working days lost per 1000 employees ranging from none to 54 (54 being an outlier).

Nissera UK was founded in 1988 as part of a strategy to serve major Japanese customers in Europe. It was located in an area in which manufacturing accounted for nearly 40 per cent of jobs. The employment trends in 1996 showed that nearly 40 per cent of the working population was employed in manufacturing as compared with nearly 19 per cent nationally. Statistics on social class by occupation in 1991 showed that the highest percentage (approximately 17 per cent) of the population in total was economically active in the managerial and technical group.

The strong manufacturing base in the West Midlands had meant a strong government initiative for inward investment in the area. The region was within the Department of Trade and Industry Regional Selective Area for assistance to businesses (Department of Trade and Industry, 1995). Furthermore, an inward investment survey, carried out in 1995, highlighted the area in which Nissera UK was located as successful in attracting foreign investment with over 60 overseas companies representing ten countries, such as AT&T Istel (US) and Heller Machine Tools (Germany). The largest number of businesses was from the United States (36 per cent in 1999). Japanese companies constituted the largest body of investment in the area (nine per cent), ranking second after the US in job creation (21 per cent).

The industrial dispute in the West Midlands was seen as much worse than in the South West region in terms of working days lost per 1000 employees through strikes and stoppages. According to the Office for National Statistics (1999), working days lost per 1000 employees between 1991 and 1998 ranged from seven to 56, compared with the industrial average of ten to 57 over the same period.

The strategic alliance between the Rover Group and Honda was formed in 1978. Rover was looking for a partner to help structure its organization and to remedy the lack of new projects, whilst Honda wanted to increase its sales volume in Europe.

At the time of the collaboration, there had been a decline in the uncompetitive British manufacturing sector, which produced dramatic changes in the level and composition of employment. For instance, between 1970 and 1983, Britain lost 2.4 million manufacturing jobs (Hirst and Zeitlin, 1989). The West Midlands, being the traditional home of Britain's car manufacturing base had taken the lion's share of this loss. Problems with management were seen as a crucial cause of the perceived manufacturing failure.

The British management problem is that, within their area of discretion, British managers consistently take poor decisions about the priority of different problems and execute their strategies in a way that is generally inept . . . Before the 1979–83 recession it was possible to blame poor organization of production on the workforce and the unions. But that excuse is no longer plausible. The organization of production inside the factory is now clearly the prerogative of management. (Hirst and Zeitlin, 1989, p. 82)

It is argued that the location of Rover's Longbridge plant in an old industrial district, which was characterized by declining heavy or primary industries, strengthened its bargaining position in view of the levels of unemployment in the area (ibid.).[2] Under this circumstance, workers could be expected to be more willing to accommodate a new workplace regime out of economic necessity.

In the 1980s, the West Midlands had witnessed an attraction of Japanese investment of mainly an FDI nature in the automotive sector. This meant a high government interest in investment in the area. There was immense government support for the Rover–Honda collaboration. For example, by 1982, 'government financing stood at £1.4 billion and there had been substantial private funding' (Autocar, 1988).

Labour relations in the West Midlands have been described as significantly worse than those in new towns, such as Telford, with high levels of industrial dispute experienced in the West Midlands over the period 1986–1993 (Sharpe, 1998). At the organizational level, there had been heavy unionization at Rover. For example, Sir Michael Edwardes, who was offered the job of executive chairman of the then named British Leyland Motor Corporation (BLMC) in 1977, 'took a tough line with the trade unions, in particular with the powerful shop stewards, who were obviously not happy about massive redundancies among their members' (British Motor Industry Heritage Trust, 1997, p. 58).

In contrast to the findings of the Japanization literature (such as Oliver and Wilkinson, 1992), this study did not find that the level of industrial disputes (in terms of the working days lost per 1000 employees through strikes and stoppages) in a region had significant impact on the degree of internalization of Japanese work systems. A low level of industrial disputes in the region in which Teniki UK was located did not facilitate the internalization of Japanese work systems. Similarly, high levels of industrial disputes in the regions in which Nissera UK and Rover were located did not impede internalization. On the contrary, the Teniki UK workforce displayed resistance to new methods of work despite the low level of industrial disputes in the area. This was due to the dominant effect of a pre-existing culture. Education and skill levels were low at Teniki UK, reflecting the fact that it was located in a tourist region without a strong manufacturing base: according to the personnel and training manager (15 February 1999), 60 per cent of employees had no more than three Graduate

Certificates for Secondary Education (GCSEs). This had a negative impact on the internalization of parent company practices.

> You have not been able to deliver the Kaizen and other activities because you have not done the fundamental training. Also the factory people around here – this is a farmland around here, so demographically it is not an engineering magnet. So we got people that have not worked in an automotive factory with all the pressures, all the technology and requirements of a Japanese company. Therefore, we need to bring the core competencies up to a level and the only way to do that is to train and educate. (British operations manager, 18 January 2000)

The pattern of low skills in the local labour market was reinforced by government regional policy. State support for inward investment was low in the tourist region in which Teniki UK was located, while it was high in the location sites of Nissera UK and Rover–Honda. This reflected the government policy of allocating resources to regions most affected by industrial restructuring and most dependent on manufacturing (Byers, 2001). The resulting low inward investment in Teniki UK's region helped maintain the low skills level of local labour compared with areas that received government support for investment. However, given that the regions with high skills in manufacturing were favourable to the adoption of continuous improvement schemes, a future increase in the skills level in less developed regions might facilitate their adoption of manufacturing philosophies and techniques.

This study also shows that location in a greenfield site, in association with high skills in manufacturing, facilitated the internalization of highly institutionalized Japanese practices, as the new workforce had fewer preconceptions (see Sharpe, 1997). Hence, a new set of work procedures could be introduced with less resistance. This was not necessarily related to the recruitment of older, experienced workers with 'a basic work ethic of attendance, obeying orders and not quitting' (Elger and Smith, 1998, p. 541; Hallier and Leopold, 2000). The argument here is not that greenfield firms are better able to impose their practices on local labour market conditions. It is that organizational factors, such as the attention paid by Japanese expatriates to the implementation of continuous improvement schemes, can play a more prominent role than local institutional factors in the internalization process. The point to note is that the impact of local institutional factors on the internalization process needs to be considered in conjunction with that of organizational factors.

In a brownfield site such as Teniki UK, organizational inertia tends to lead to practices that more closely resemble local practices. To a degree this also applies to Rover–Honda. Strong lines of demarcation at Rover led to the defence of job territory and challenged the drive toward increased flexibility in the manufacturing area. However, the engineers, on whom this study focuses, showed less resistance to the internalization of Japanese work systems owing to the different nature of their work, skills base and learning resulting from the previous collaborative work with Honda.

Thus the degree of internalization of Japanese work systems tends to be high where there is a favourable local institutional context, characterized by high inward investment and location on a greenfield site, as at Nissera UK. In addition, the absence of a pre-existing culture is more conducive to the internalization of Japanese work systems than a non-unionized labour market. In other words, location in a region with a high level of industrial disputes and a strong manufacturing base is not necessarily an obstacle to the internalization of alternative work systems where there is a large supply of skilled labour, as illustrated by the Rover–Honda case. In contrast to previous research (for example Elger and Smith, 1994), a large supply of unskilled workers and location in a tourist region (as with Teniki UK), where labour can be expected to be relatively free of preconceived ideas in manufacturing, do not facilitate the internalization of Japanese work systems. Thus the local institutional factors that are of significance here are skills levels, type of industrial base and state support for investment. The key national and local institutional characteristics are summarized in Table 4.2.

Table 4.2   Key national and local institutional characteristics

Context		Teniki UK	Nissera UK	Rover–Honda R8/YY Project
Local institutional context	*Location site*	Brownfield	Greenfield	Home of Britain's traditional car manufacturing base
	Area	Centre for tourism	Centre for manufacturing	
	Skills base	Low in manufacturing	High in manufacturing	Medium in engineering*
	Inward investment	Low	High	High
	Level of industrial conflict†	Low	High	High
National institutional context	Institutional gap between the compartmentalized UK business system and the highly coordinated Japanese business system Variation in emphasis on tacit and explicit work systems between Japan and the UK			

Notes:
* Perceived level in comparison to that of Honda
† Working days lost per 1000 employees

Organizational Context

The nature of the relationship of Teniki UK's previous owner (ABC Ltd., a pseudonym) under a joint venture agreement with Teniki was such that ABC Ltd. provided the production facility and the local management team, and Teniki provided the technical expertise. 'It [the joint venture] was run by a group of directors with limited sales. They ran the operation in terms of production lines, very limited product types going through' (British operations manager, 18 January 2000). The joint venture performed poorly with low quality standards and efficiency levels.

Before its acquisition, Teniki UK's organizational culture was claimed to be ingrained in fire-fighting and poor management–worker relations. Older operators worked in a non-informative environment characterized by poor communication and weak control. 'ABC Ltd. did not have anything in terms of Statistical Process Controls (SPCs) etcetera. They had no set standards. Japanese brought them as they came' (British human resource officer, 29 July 1999). Promises of training were made, but rarely delivered. Training focused on teaching skills related to an operator's immediate task. Operators were not introduced to an integrated manufacturing process.

Teniki UK's senior management was replaced with a more market-oriented, quality-conscious team upon its acquisition. Since 1996, six Japanese advisors had been brought into Teniki UK from the parent company. They acted as technical experts in the technical and development, operations, and sales and marketing areas, avoiding positions of direct control in the management hierarchy. The people side of management was left to local managers.

The greenfield case company, Nissera UK, was financially more stable and less dependent on its parent company than Teniki UK. It had been in operation since 1988 and had attempted an organizational restructuring as a cost-saving measure in 1997. The composition of the senior management team changed in the years after its foundation from 60 per cent Japanese employees initially to the current six per cent. In all, 12 Japanese managers (two senior directors, eight managers in engineering and two managers in the functional area) served liaison roles between the subsidiary and the parent company. The production managers and supervisors were predominantly British and recruited locally. 'From the start, the workforce was all local. Management structure was mostly Japanese. From day one, it was planned that British managers would be selected to fill in the roles occupied by the Japanese over time' (British production manager, 30 July 1999).

At the start of the Rover–Honda collaboration, the two companies had comparable sales volumes. However, Honda was profitable and growing rapidly, while Rover was loss-making and some of its previous projects had damaged the company's image.

Honda had the characteristic Japanese TQC attitude to manufacturing, which was diffused to Rover over a lengthy tuition period. According to Faulkner (1995), Honda had the technology to gain the necessary cost economies and the financial strength to collaborate with Rover in the production of new models. 'There was the recognition within the British Leyland Group that we were a small company in what is a huge market and that we could not financially afford to go developing new cars on our own. So I think we were mostly financially driven' (principal electrical engineer G, 12 May 1999).

The R8/YY project was a turning point for the company in financial terms, marking the initiation of structural and cultural change at Rover. 'The success of the model in the market place made a significant contribution to returning Rover to financial profitability. The extent of learning from Honda also reached a peak during the period of R8/YY manufacture' (see Appendix VI for the benefit scale).

In line with the literature (for example Fligstein, 1990), the case study companies' pre-existing strategies, structures and technologies shape the pattern of change toward the 'Japanese model'. Actual practices do not conform to the prescriptions implemented in Japan, and diffused work systems are renegotiated and adapted. Although all three firms found it difficult to develop and replicate *esprit de corps*, Nissera UK and Rover were relatively more successful in implementing a team-based structure and continuous improvement activities such as quality circles. In Nissera UK, the team structure had been in place for some time, the workforce was more skilled and the parent company provided long-term financing. In contrast to Teniki UK, Japanese managers at Nissera UK offered hands-on training to older operators and were heavily involved in shop-floor activities. In other words, Japanese expatriates attempted to carry over to the UK the characteristic Japanese pattern of institutional co-operation (see for example Orrù, 1997).

At Nissera UK, management had a strong approach to discipline until 1997, which marked the end of the Japanese managing director's (with a production engineering background) employment contract.[3] The attention paid to the implementation of continuous improvement schemes, in addition to the availability of financial and human resources, meant that the level of commitment to such schemes was higher at Nissera UK than at Teniki UK. At Nissera UK, hands-on training of operators by the Japanese in the early years resembled the master–apprentice relationship in which 'craft' skills were acquired, 'not through language but through observation, imitation and practice' (Nonaka and Takeuchi, 1995, p. 63). However,

Japanese management's training, supervisory and advisory roles diminished over the years as the phase of implementing new management systems and practices was completed. Subsequently, with the replacement of Japanese expatriates by local management, less attention was paid to continuous improvement principles: 'Although they had more strict rules, Japanese managers would help you work. They would go to the source of the problem. British managers make up titles and waste money' (operator in car component manufacture at Nissera UK). The role of actors in shaping alternative systems was particularly visible where there was a lack of management initiative in emphasizing training and adopting a strong approach to discipline.

Teniki UK had not yet achieved economies of scale and this put financial pressure on local management in its efforts to impart continuous improvement philosophies to operators. Moreover, 57 per cent of its parent company's shares were held by a Japanese car manufacturer – Teniki's biggest customer. This arrangement further constrained Teniki UK's flexibility. Given its recent acquisition, the UK subsidiary had not been under Japanese ownership long enough to be fully imbued with a continuous improvement culture.

The cases demonstrate that the nature of Japanese management intervention in the implementation of diffused work systems is crucial in shaping the internalization process. In particular, whether management involvement in meeting strategic and operational aims is hands-on or indirect, and the degree of involvement of Japanese expatriate management in strategic and operational decisions (including supervision on the shop floor) are factors influencing how the adopter firm perceives the exercise of control by the source firm. This in turn shapes actors' decisions on whether to accept new ideas. Corporate acculturation in this sense is based on developing informal networks of communication whereby international ethos and practices of the parent firm can be observed (see Martinez and Jarillo, 1989).

In line with the arguments in the literature (for example, Lincoln and Kalleberg, 1990), large organizations can offer greater financial resources for the implementation and internalization of Japanese work systems than small organizations. For example, the Rover–Honda collaboration's large size and the associated economies of scale in production allowed more resources to be allocated to the employee training necessary for the internalization of alternative work practices. By the same token, the passage of time (11 years at Nissera UK and Rover–Honda sites from the year of foundation to the time of data collection or project completion) and the experience of a previous working relationship encouraged emphasis on worker training and learning. For example, the secondment of Rover engineers to

Japan for six to 12 months, the establishment of a liaison office in 1985 and joint engineering team meetings with Honda engineers facilitated the implementation and internalization of Honda's continuous improvement techniques and philosophies at Rover.

Personal relations and the accompanying trust embedded in social networks were important means by which Rover acquired and shared tacit knowledge. Company visits and boundary-spanning individuals encouraged socialization, allowing tacit knowledge to be acquired through experience (see for example Nonaka and Takeuchi, 1995). Habitual routines were redesigned in order to integrate Honda practices. Some of the integration mechanisms involved staff dedicated to the development of the collaboration, enabling coordination through lateral communication and negotiation rather than hierarchy. Furthermore, inter-personal, inter-firm networks were used for coordination and integration (see for example Grandori and Soda, 1995). Nevertheless, the interpretation and use of Honda practices were far from smooth. It was difficult to break 'method[s that were] embedded in individual expression' (manufacturing integration manager at Rover, 25 August 1999). Doing so necessitated intensive training. There was a high level of training in quality skills and car development systems at Rover. Direct involvement with the Japanese and emphasis on training by local management were two means of avoiding the 'watering down' of Honda practices. However, the diffusion of know-how from Honda to Rover was not as smooth as that to Honda's wholly owned subsidiary in the US. This was partly the result of issues of commercial confidentiality. Thus, while Rover engineers could be shown the assembly line or order of tasks for a given process, they could not receive any information on measurements or dimensions. Honda felt that such information was too sensitive to be disclosed to technical collaborators, for the two companies were competing in the same markets.

Both Nissera UK and Rover–Honda invested considerable effort in diffusing tacit and explicit components of continuous improvement schemes by providing financial resources and employing high numbers of Japanese expatriates in the early years of operation. The cases indicate that tacit philosophies such as 'team spirit' were more difficult for the UK workforce to internalize than explicit techniques such as team-based structures.

The key company and organizational characteristics that have an impact on the diffusion process across the three firms are summarized in Table 4.3.

In Chapter One, an analytic framework had been constructed about the impact of key institutional and organizational characteristics on the degree of implementation and internalization of Japanese knowledge-driven work systems. Figure 4.2 summarizes the results of the match between the analytic framework and the empirical findings.

Table 4.3 Key company and organizational characteristics

Characteristic	Teniki UK	Nissera UK	Rover–Honda R8/YY Project
Size (in 1999)	Medium (170 employees)	Medium (300 employees)	Large (~39,000 employees)
Age (year of acquisition or establishment)	1996–99	1988–99	1978–89
Nature of work	Assembly of car components (Factory workers)	Assembly of car components (Factory workers)	Automobile design, engineering and manufacture
Form of ownership	Subsidiary, 57 per cent of parent company shares held by Japanese car manufacturer	Subsidiary	Technical collaboration, 20 per cent mutual shareholding arrangement in 1990
Financial orientation	Short term	Long term	Long term
Number of Japanese expatriates and roles in the UK	4 (MD is British). Advisory role	12 (including MD). Mainly director role	Regular visits by Honda engineers (1986–99), liaison office established in 1985. Advisory role
Workforce skills level	Low	Medium	Medium (compared with Honda)
Nature of and emphasis on training	Hands-off, low	Hands-on, high (until 1997) and medium thereafter	Hands-on, high in quality skills and car development system
Employee commitment to diffused work systems	Low	Medium	Medium
Degree of Japanese involvement	High, indirect	High, direct	High, direct
Nature of diffused work systems	Emphasis on explicit practices (i.e. shift to team structure)	Emphasis on both tacit and explicit practices	Emphasis on both tacit and explicit practices

Figure 4.2 shows that, at the national level, structural and cultural lega-cies of Japan and the UK can influence the degree to which Japanese knowledge-driven work systems are implemented and, ultimately, inter-nalized by UK adopter firms. At the local institutional level, location site and area, inward investment and skills base of labour have an impact on the implementation and internalization of work systems. The level of industrial dispute is not found to have a significant influence on the imple-mentation and internalization of work systems, hence is excluded in Figure 4.2. At the level of the organization, company characteristics, the nature of diffused work systems, the emphasis placed on explicit and tacit components of these systems and the commitment displayed by the work-force towards the organizational practices of the source firm can hinder or facilitate the implementation and internalization of knowledge-driven work systems.

The findings suggest that the interaction between the local institutional and organizational levels is a two-way process. There is reciprocal interde-pendence rather than a one-way determinism. The solid arrows in between the three levels in Figure 4.2 point to the influence of each level on the one below it. For example, Rosenzweig and Nohria (1994: 234) see 'the extent to which [the company] is subject to pressure from local institutions such as unions and governmental bodies' as having an impact on human resource practices. This points to the impact of the local institutional level on the organizational level. The broken arrows in the figure represent 'trickling-up' impact[4] of the local practices on higher levels of analysis such as the industrial relations system, the system of training workers and man-agers, internal structure of corporate firms, structured relationships among firms in the same industry as well as their suppliers and customers, and idio-syncratic customs and traditions (see Hollingsworth and Boyer, 1997). The local institutional level has an impact on the actions of the local actors through a set of institutional rules, and is, in turn, influenced by incremen-tal changes in the rule systems of a subset of local actors. For instance, Teniki UK's efforts to raise the NVQ level of its workforce contribute to the enhancement of the skills base in the region.

Similarly, the internalization of work systems can have an impact on the subsequent implementation of alternative work systems. 'The users make significant and extensive contributions to the eventual shape and uses of an innovation' (Clark, 1987, p.169). The routinization of knowledge-driven work systems can create a path-dependency that has an effect on the sub-sequent introduction of alternative work systems. This research focuses on single flows of influence from higher levels of analysis to lower levels. The reverse flows are not investigated. Future research is needed to investigate the impact of local practices on the local institutional and national levels,

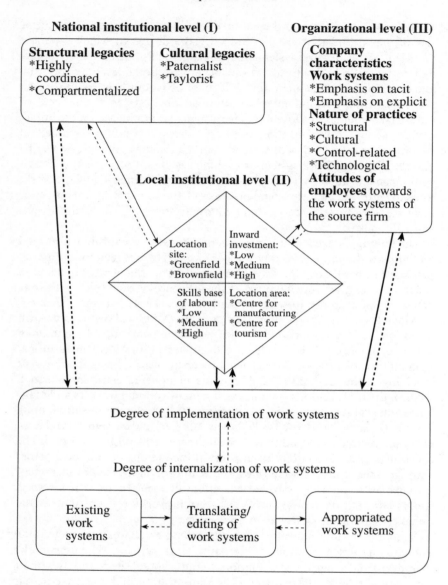

Figure 4.2 The impact of macro- and micro-influences on work systems diffusion

as well as the impact of internalized work systems on the implementation process (see Chapter Five).

3. REVISIT TO THE PROPOSITIONS

In Chapter Two, five propositions had been formulated about the combined influence of nationally and locally distinct institutional settings on the implementation and internalization of Japanese knowledge-driven work systems. These propositions run across a scale marked by distinct combinations of favourable and/or unfavourable key institutional and organizational characteristics that are likely to have an impact on the implementation and internalization of Japanese work systems in varying degrees. Propositions 1 and 2 represent the extreme points on the scale. Propositions 3 to 5 cover the possible impact of intermediate institutional settings on the degree of implementation and internalization. The propositions are iterated with follow-up discussions below.

Proposition 1
 Affiliates of MNCs in highly institutionalized environments that are operating in unfavourable institutional settings overseas (as those delineated in Table 2.3) are likely to exhibit a low degree of implementation and internalization of MNC work systems.

Proposition 2
 Affiliates of MNCs in highly institutionalized environments that are operating in favourable institutional settings overseas (as those delineated in Table 2.3) are likely to exhibit a high degree of implementation and internalization of MNC work systems.

These two propositions, which represent 'ideal' states, are not observed in the cases examined. They can be tested through future research on cross-national comparison of the diffusion of work systems in Japan and the UK (see Chapter Five). The same applies to Proposition 5.

Proposition 5
 Incoherent pattern of high and low degree of implementation and internalization is likely to develop in settings which lack key institutional and organizational characteristics that are favourable or unfavourable.

As the three cases display 'intermediate' settings, where some of the favourable key institutional and organizational characteristics are more dominant than unfavourable ones, the fifth claim cannot be tested here. This also calls for future research. However, the combined research findings across the three sites indicate that shifts in the nature of institutional and organizational characteristics can lead to changes in the degree of implementation and internalization of knowledge-driven work systems.

Proposition 3

  Affiliates of MNCs in highly institutionalized environments that are operating in settings in which unfavourable key institutional and organizational characteristics are more dominant than the favourable ones are likely to exhibit a low degree of implementation and internalization of MNC work systems.

The research findings at Teniki UK support this claim. The nature of business system typified by a 'compartmentalized' structural legacy and a 'Taylorist' cultural legacy is representative of Teniki UK's national institutional context. The diffusion of Japanese knowledge-driven work systems is negatively influenced by the company's location on a brownfield site in a centre for tourism (which provides a low skills base in manufacturing, hence needs to be taken as unfavourable rather than favourable in this context).[5] Moreover, there is a large supply of unskilled workers in the area (which is also taken here as unfavourable rather than favourable). Teniki UK management focuses on diffusing explicit practices. The commitment to continuous improvement schemes is low. These multilevel characteristics in combination tend to be more dominant than the positive impact that a low industrial dispute in the region can have on the implementation and internalization of work systems.

Proposition 4

  Affiliates of MNCs in highly institutionalized environments that are operating in settings in which favourable key institutional and organizational characteristics are more dominant than the unfavourable ones are likely to exhibit a high degree of implementation and internalization of MNC work systems.

There is strong evidence from the case studies to suggest that the extent to which alternative work systems are accepted is higher at Nissera UK than at Teniki UK. The local institutional setting of Nissera UK is marked by a large supply of skilled workers (taken as favourable in this context as opposed to what was delineated in Table 2.3 in Chapter Two) and location on a greenfield site with a high inward investment. Moreover, the company is located in a centre for manufacturing, which tends to be preferable for

Japanese management owing to the fact that the workforce has the basic skills necessary for fundamental training in continuous improvement schemes. The national institutional environment is not characterized by a 'highly coordinated' organizational structure and a 'paternalist' organizational culture given that the firm is located in the UK business system. Nonetheless, favourable key local institutional and organizational characteristics, such as heavy emphasis on cultural and control-related practices or tacit work systems, as well as a medium level of commitment to continuous improvement schemes, are more dominant than the unfavourable characteristics. An analysis of the national institutional setting alone would have led to a conclusion that the degree of internalized work systems is low.

The Rover–Honda case has a similar institutional make-up to that of Teniki UK in terms of its embeddedness in a 'compartmentalized business' system and the existence of pre-established work routines. However, Rover's emphasis on both tacit and explicit knowledge over the course of the R8/YY project, a high skills base in engineering, high inward investment and key organizational strategies dominate to yield a medium level internalization of Honda systems.

It should be noted that a high level of implementation of alternative work systems is not necessarily associated with a high level of internalization. The Nissera UK and Rover case studies indicate that despite high levels of implementation, the internalization of Japanese work systems is medium. Future research can shed light upon the characteristics that are likely to have an impact on the level of implementation alone, separate from those that are likely to influence the level of internalization (see Chapter Five).

4. THE INSTITUTIONAL LIMITS TO DIFFUSION OF WORK SYSTEMS

The findings at Teniki UK, Nissera UK and the Rover–Honda collaboration reveal that there are considerable differences in the diffusion of Japanese work systems across the brownfield, greenfield and technical collaboration sites in the same sector owing to two barriers: (i) the differences in type of capitalist system and (ii) the variation in emphasis on tacit and explicit work systems between Japan and the UK.

Embeddedness at the National Level

At the national level, the operational autonomy provided to individuals in small-group activities strengthened by a sense of groupism in large firms in the Japanese automotive industry conflicts with the low worker discretion and sense of individualism that has traditionally strengthened the management hierarchy in the UK automotive industry. The experience of developing interdependency, trust and shared knowledge is unique to a specific workplace, context and group of people (Cutcher-Gershenfeld et al., 1998). Thus, all three companies in the sample had difficulty imparting continuous improvement activities by securing the commitment of all parties to the process owing to the institutional variation between the demands of a highly coordinated business system that encourages strong networks of mutual obligation and commitment and a compartmentalized business system that discourages collaboration and cooperation. The degree of internalization of Japanese source companies' practices was high where pre-existing organizational settings were redesigned to integrate alternative work systems through company visits, cross-functional teamwork and the active role of Japanese expatriates as boundary-spanning individuals. As Tsang (2001) shows, the coaching role of expatriate managers is crucial in cases where substantial cognitive change is required. For example, the heavy use of expatriates at Nissera UK served as one of the ways to bring the firm into the fold, that is, to establish an organizational culture that aligned with the parent company's values (see Jaeger, 1983). In comparison, Teniki UK had the least number of Japanese expatriates available for training who tended to be hands-off in management. Hence, the resistance to alternative work systems was the greatest among Teniki UK operators. This was in part associated with particularly older operators' preference for the traditional British work organization of union activity and craftsmanship. 'We need the trade union down here to improve the work environment' (senior operator in Air Element at Teniki UK). In line with Tsang's (2001) argument, old routines hampered the diffusion of knowledge.

Embeddedness at the Organizational Level

At the organizational level, the difference in emphasis placed on explicit and tacit knowledge between Japan and the UK tends to hinder the diffusability of work systems from Japan to the UK. In line with Liker et al.'s (1999, p. 23) argument, '[T]he tacitness of much knowledge that underpins the production system imparts a marked path-dependent and firm-specific quality to the development of these systems.' For instance, findings at Teniki UK point to the need to diffuse explicit knowledge such as team-based structure in conjunction with tacit knowledge such as quality control philosophies of team spirit and work discipline. The process of enculturating team spirit is more difficult to articulate than change in authority relations along a team-based structure. Where practices are likely to have behavioural consequences such as in ways of working and interrelating or to initiate systemic change in Child and Rodrigues' (1996) terms, the internalization of work systems is more difficult. The internalization of continuous improvement schemes is much easier where they can be codified or structured into a set of identifiable rules and procedures such as Honda's project-based work organization rather than the sense of discipline required to carry out *gebba-kais*. These practices basically are techniques that do not require a major change to either people's behaviour or the pattern of relationships between them (see Child, 1994). In accordance with Ackroyd et al.'s (1988) view, initiatives mediated by the orientation of British management are less straightforward in their effects. The Japanese emphasis on the human element of knowledge production at the operational level is not upheld by the UK managers who tend to emphasize knowledge that is easy to measure and control.

Fundamentally, the different values of the Japanese source firm and the UK adopter firm in each case expose differences between individuals. According to Blackler (1995) and Swan (1999), such an exposure may lead to conflict, and the creation of new knowledge. The negotiation of work systems in this context occurs through interactive social networking rather than linear flow of information. The role of actors in facilitating the diffusion of knowledge also needs to be considered. In the cases concerned, Japanese expatriates act as a link to the source of information at the Japanese parent/partner firms, and are an effective medium for 'acquiring and encoding timely, current, and soft information' (Tushman and Scanlan, 1981: 290). For example, Rover liaison engineers helped locate expertise at Honda, and forge good working relations with the Japanese. The high level of social networking helped minimize communication problems.

The degree of internalization of Japanese work systems at UK adopter firms depends on the type of activities or the nature of diffused practices, availability of physical, financial and human resources, and level of interaction between the actors involved, in other words the role of boundary-spanning individuals in the diffusion process (see Figure 4.3).

Figure 4.3 shows the interplay of actors, resources and activities within a social network that is necessary to sustain the internalization of Japanese work systems in the given cases. There is a greater likelihood of Japanese work systems being internalized by UK adopter firms where actors at different levels interact intensely to diffuse work systems, and heterogeneous – physical, financial and human – resources are available to support structural, cultural, control-related and technological components of continuous improvement schemes. Team-based structures, quality circles, 5C housekeeping principles and the exercise of control through visibility in management are perceived as standardized models to be imitated in the

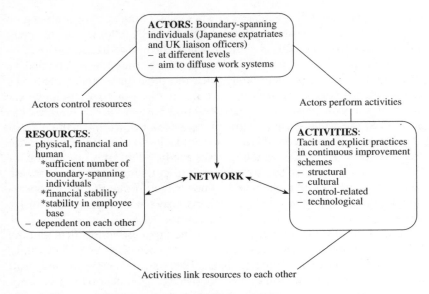

Source: Figure structure adapted from Håkansson (1986)

Figure 4.3   *Network framework conducive to high internalization of work systems*

absence of resources and actors aiming to diffuse both tacit and explicit practices. The network framework in this figure gives one the context in which to understand the decisions that managers have to take and the adopters' response to those decisions. It should be noted that the focus here is more on networking relations and less on network structures that Håkansson (1986) highlights in his work. The findings in this study emphasize structure as well as agency.

5. SUMMARY

This chapter discussed findings from the case studies on the implementation and internalization of Japanese knowledge-driven work systems in two UK subsidiary firms and an Anglo-Japanese technical collaboration in the automotive manufacturing industry. It highlighted the variation in the degree of implementation and internalization of Japanese work systems that reflected locally distinct settings across the brownfield (Teniki UK), greenfield (Nissera UK) and technical (Rover-Honda) collaboration sites. The extent to which work systems were implemented and internalized contrasted greatly between Teniki UK and the combined findings at Nissera UK and the Rover–Honda collaboration along the following key dimensions: the local institutional characteristics, such as location site and area and inward investment; the company size and age and terms of financing; the nature of diffused practices; and workforce attitudes. It is argued here that work systems are embedded at the national and organizational levels. The empirical findings support the third, fourth and fifth propositions. In other words key national and local institutional and organizational characteristics have predominantly high or low impact on the degree of implementation and internalization of knowledge-driven work systems.

NOTES

1. This support was in the form of delegating responsibility for the assembly of the high value-added component to Nissera UK. In addition, Nissera engineers were dispatched to the UK plant to increase productivity, and to reduce 'quality failure cost'.
2. The unemployment levels in West Midlands and Great Britain as a whole (nine per cent) have been consistently higher than those in, for example, the Telford work area (7.8 per cent) (Wrekin Council, 1994 in Sharpe, 1998).
3. The Japanese managing director (MD) with a production engineering background was succeeded by an MD with a finance background.
4. The term 'trickling-up' is used to denote the assertion that the impact may not be observed immediately in the short run.
5. Location in a centre dominated by the service industry was expected to limit the implementation and internalization of work systems (see Table 2.3 in Chapter Two).

5. Conclusions, implications and limitations

This concluding chapter presents a review of the key findings that are fed back to the central research question. In addition, the implications of research findings for theory development and practice are discussed. Attention is also paid to the limitations of this study. Lastly, an agenda for future research is presented and closing remarks are made.

1. THE CENTRAL ROLE OF APPROPRIATION IN DIFFUSION

The degree of implementation and internalization of knowledge-driven work systems in three Japanese affiliate firms in the UK automotive manufacturing sector are described, analysed and compared (see Chapter Four). In this context, work systems are taken as continuous improvement activities that are driven by people's tacit knowledge as well as the explicit structural and technological systems (see Chapter One). The diffusion of work systems is seen as incorporating people management (or management intervention) as well as the internalization of these work systems by users (see Chapter One). This process is examined in relation to, first, the institutional embeddedness of work systems at the national level and, second, the embeddedness of tacit aspects of work systems at the firm level. The macro-level embeddedness is understood as the shaping of work systems by structural and cultural understandings of a country, which constitute distinct business systems. Japanese and UK business systems represent 'highly coordinated' and 'compartmentalized' business environments respectively (see Chapter Two). The highly coordinated business systems and paternalist cultural legacies of firms tend to limit the diffusability of work systems. In other words, the embeddedness of Japanese firms in distinct institutional settings challenges the diffusability of their work systems to other institutional settings. The micro-level embeddedness is taken as the extent to which work systems are bound to tight networks of social relations, whereby the emphasis rests more on tacit than explicit knowledge. The emphasis on tacit aspects of work systems is also discussed here as limiting the diffusability of work systems (see Chapter Two). As the case studies indicate, there is a tendency for UK management to show interest in the diffusion of structure and techniques as opposed to a complex set of meanings attached to work systems. There have been efforts, such as those of the DTI with the Towards Integration Programme launched in 1987, to increase awareness of UK management towards philosophies rather than technology as key to Japanese competitors' success. In spite of such efforts, processes of adoption in the UK still seem to be characterized by a diffusion of one or two particular management techniques in isolation from the broader strategy and philosophy of lean production.

The degree of implementation and internalization of Japanese work systems has been addressed with regard to the nature and relevance of local institutional and organizational characteristics. The location site and area and the associated skills base are taken as key local institutional characteristics. Strong government support for investment in the region (constituting another local institutional characteristic) is seen as encouraging the diffusion of quality management standards to and the enhancement of skills at the UK adopter firms. At the organizational level, company size, age and terms of financing, the nature of and level of commitment to diffused practices are seen as influencing the implementation and internalization of work systems (see Chapters One and Four). Based on the review of the literature, along the dimensions of the nature and historical roots of social institutions, on Japanization, innovation processes, and neo-institutionalism, debates on the user-oriented perspective within the innovation processes literature and the historical neo-institutional perspective within the neo-institutional literature are seen as appropriate in identifying a list of key national and organizational characteristics that are influential in the diffusion of work systems. The social institutions operating at a national level include the state, financial system, public training system, legal system, authority relations and union strength. In terms of cultural legacies, the following aspects are regarded as significant in shaping the diffusion of work systems: task fragmentation, worker discretion and involvement, managerial control of work organization, separation of managers from workers and employer commitment to employment security (see Chapters One and Two). At the organizational level, the role of actors in editing alternative practices at adopter firms is highlighted. The worker response to alternative work systems, incorporating their values and interests, is acknowledged in an effort to consider the social patterns shaping the diffusion process (see Chapters One and Four).

Teniki UK, Nissera UK and the Rover-Honda collaboration in the automotive industry exemplify the way in which firms draw only selectively upon production practices associated with the 'Japanese model'.

Compromise solutions are common in which only explicit aspects of the Japanese model are adopted (see Delbridge, 1998), and conflicting institutional legacies hinder the diffusability of work systems. The brownfield site displayed a relatively low degree of implementation as well as low internalization of Japanese work systems. By contrast, the greenfield and technical collaboration sites had a high degree of implementation and a medium level of internalization owing to the availability of more financial and human (that is, Japanese expatriate) resources, direct and high involvement by Japanese management, the exercise of direct personal and cultural control and provision of hands-on training, longer period in operation and higher skills levels (see Table 5.1 for an overview of the results).

The findings highlight the structural and processual limits to the diffusion of Japanese work systems. The research points to the following influences on work-systems diffusion: the characteristics of the adopter firm; the nature of diffused systems; and the institutional context to which work systems belong. The combined influence of the national and local institutional and organizational characteristics differs greatly across the three cases. At Teniki UK, the local institutional environment is not supportive of a high level of internalization of Japanese knowledge-driven work systems. The location of the company on a brownfield site in a centre for tourism is challenging the acceptance of alternative work systems. The emphasis on tourism in the region creates a low skills base in manufacturing, which is not found to be favourable to imparting continuous improvement principles to operators at Teniki UK. In addition to the large supply of unskilled workers, there is low inward investment and an emphasis by management on the diffusion of structural practices and continuous improvement techniques. There is also a low level of commitment by workers to such techniques. The low level of commitment is associated with the conflict between pre-existing group norms and those required by the new practices. Teniki UK's limited financial and human resources and emphasis on explicit practices in continuous improvement schemes tend to hinder efforts to sustain high levels of acceptance of such schemes among operators. Work systems are translated by workers who are accustomed to an alternative organizational routine and adhere to group norms that are different from those expected by the Japanese.

The local institutional environment of Nissera UK is considerably more supportive of the internalization of Japanese work systems. The combined influence of key institutional and organizational characteristics encourages a higher degree of internalization of work systems at Nissera UK than Teniki UK. The company is located on a greenfield site in a centre for manufacturing. This is an area marked by a large supply of skilled workers, providing Japanese management with the foundation necessary for operators

Table 5.1 Summary of the diffusion outcomes and key institutional and organizational characteristics in play

Degree of implementation and internalization		Teniki UK	Nissera UK	Rover–Honda R8/YY Project
	Implementation	Low	High	High
	Internalization	Low	Medium	Medium
		⇑	⇑	⇑
Key national and local institutional characteristics		UK business system characterized by unfavourable compartmentalized structural legacy Taylorist cultural legacy Emphasis on explicit knowledge		
Key organizational characteristics	Location site, area Skills base and inward investment	Brownfield. Centre for tourism Low Low	Greenfield. Centre for manufacturing High High	Traditional manufacturing base Medium High
	Company size, age (from establishment to data collection/end of project) and terms of financing	Medium 3 years Short-term orientation	Medium 11 years Long-term orientation	Large 11 years (to the completion of the R8/YY project) Long-term orientation
	Employee commitment to diffused work systems	Low	Medium	Medium
	Emphasis on the nature of diffused work systems	Explicit structural practices	Tacit cultural, control-related and explicit structural practices	Tacit cultural, control-related and explicit structural, technological practices

Source: Chapter Four

to grasp continuous improvement techniques and philosophies. A sufficient number of Japanese expatriates work in the subsidiary to diffuse both tacit and explicit practices in continuous improvement schemes. They work within a context of financial stability. There is also a higher level of commitment to alternative work systems than at Teniki UK. Given the absence of any tradition of manufacturing under British ownership and the long period spent in operation under Japanese ownership, Nissera UK workers demonstrate a higher level of internalization of the principles of teamwork and self-discipline in improving process efficiency and product quality than their counterparts at Teniki UK.

The institutional make-up of the Rover–Honda collaboration does not seem encouraging at first glance. The location of the UK partner in a centre for traditional British manufacturing can be expected to hinder the diffusion process, as pre-institutionalized group norms and organizational routines conflict with the requirements of alternative work systems. For example, the management system of Rover did not provide much 'independence' to individuals or work groups prior to the company's collaboration with Honda. The widely-perceived Japanese characteristic of commitment to small-group activities was not widely followed by Rover workers. However, the management initiatives of establishing a liaison office, shifting to a project-based structure and emphasizing work discipline, training, trust formation, and commitment to joint engineering in 1985 encouraged the acceptance of Honda practices by Rover engineers. The research findings show that the interplay of actors, resources and activities is more noticeable in the technical collaboration site than it is in the brownfield site due to the direct involvement of actors and availability of resources in the diffusion of both tacit and explicit systems.

The influence of nationally distinct social institutions that show divergence in business systems *across* countries, local institutions that point to divergence *within* a particular business system, and organizational characteristics that highlight the role of actors (management initiatives and interpretation of alternative work systems by adopters) is reflected in the degree of implementation and internalization across Teniki UK, Nissera UK and the Rover–Honda collaboration (the R8/YY project). At the organizational level, the highly context-dependent Japanese work systems can be blended and redesigned upon their diffusion to a different national business system. At the national level, those work systems that are close to the institutional norms and practices of the adopter firms may be more widely diffused. In contrast to isomorphism and convergence arguments (see for example DiMaggio and Powell, 1991), adopter firms do not necessarily mimic a particular work system that they consider highly effective and efficient. Firms attempt locally to interpret diffused work systems rather than submit to environmental pressures toward isomorphism. Incompatibility in institutionalized patterns of operating is not shaped by technical efficiency criteria alone.

With a focus on organizational action based on a collective apparatus of sense-making, it is argued here that appropriation is an inherent part of the diffusion process. Meanings ascribed to and derived from alternative work systems are edited in accordance with situational circumstances and constraints. Thus, it would not be germane to argue that pressures towards isomorphism induce acceptance of the same practices all over the world. The variation in outcomes is not just a matter of the speed of diffusion depending on the institutional context and structural position of each country, but adopters' interpretative mechanisms. The actual processes of organizing reveal greater heterogeneity than that found by looking at presentations or labels used for various forms, reforms and practices. As Sahlin-Andersson (1996, p. 80) contends, '[A]s a specific course of events emerges as exemplary for many very different situations, it is disconnected from time and place and forms a context-free prototype.' In a new setting, these events are reformulated in the light of various contingencies, limitations and obstacles.

In Response to the Central Research Question

The research findings enable the formulation of the following answers to the central research question:

> What is the impact of national and local institutional variation on the diffusion of work systems in multinational corporations' internationalization efforts?

Firms are embedded in both national and local institutional contexts which are comprised of a range of distinct characteristics that are either favourable or unfavourable to the development of particular degrees of implementation and internalization. The empirical findings at Teniki UK show that the combined influences of nationally distinct structural and cultural legacies and local institutional and organizational characteristics are unfavourable to the implementation and internalization of Japanese work systems. At Teniki UK, the combination of a compartmentalized structural legacy and a Taylorist cultural legacy with location on a brownfield site in a centre for tourism is found to have a negative impact on the diffusion of work systems. The low degree of implementation and internalization of work systems is also related to a large supply of unskilled workers, low inward investment in the region, an emphasis by management on the diffusion of explicit practices and a low level of worker commitment. By contrast, despite an unfavourable national business system, the combined influence of favourable local institutional and organizational characteristics is found to facilitate the diffusion of Japanese work systems to Nissera UK and the Rover–Honda collaboration. At Nissera UK, the combined influences of a large supply of skilled workers, location on a greenfield site in a centre for manufacturing, high inward investment; heavy emphasis by management on explicit and tacit practices and a medium level of worker commitment tend to facilitate the implementation and internalization of Japanese knowledge-driven work systems. The positive influence of an emphasis on both tacit and explicit practices, and high skills base and high inward investment in the area on the diffusion process also applies to the Rover–Honda collaboration site. The impact of these three characteristics is more dominant than that of Rover's location site. The time element in working with alternative methods strengthens the impact of the three characteristics. It should be noted that both Nissera UK and the Rover–Honda collaboration are older sites than Teniki UK.

The empirical evidence found in this study underpins the conclusion that the relative ease with which work systems of multinational corporations are implemented and internalized by adopter firms varies with the nationally and locally distinct nature of a range of key institutional and organizational characteristics.

2.   THEORETICAL IMPLICATIONS

The case study findings contribute to the debate on the divergence of capitalist systems (see for example Campbell et al., 1991; Hollingsworth and Boyer, 1997); they do not support the argument that convergence is taking place in response to the pressures of globalization. At the same time, the study differs from existing observations in the literature on neo-institutionalism in that empirical evidence is provided on different regional institutional systems within the UK. There is 'persistent differentiation' when local institutional differences and the role of actors at the organizational level are taken into consideration. In other words, the diffusion process, even though under the influence of the same national institutional characteristics, is specific to the given sites.

With continuing national institutional diversity, variations in the implementation and internalization of Japanese work systems between source and adopter firms can be expected to persist. However, the impact of national institutional diversity on the diffusion of work systems needs to be considered in conjunction with local institutional diversity and organizational initiative. For instance, in institutional contexts where there is a strong emphasis on non-unionism and performance-based pay systems, as in the US, the level of industrial disputes would not be expected to explain local variations in the implementation and internalization of Japanese work systems. The reshaping of alternative work systems in a new institutional setting rests on differences between practices that are embedded in distinct local and national contexts, as well as organizational factors such as workforce characteristics, financial stability and managerial emphasis on the nature of diffused work systems.

The case study findings contribute to historical neo-institutionalism by highlighting the historical influences of a business system on the subsequent development of institutional arrangements and the associated limits to homogenization of ways of operating. The findings also demonstrate the importance of actors and agency in the diffusion of work systems. Highly context-dependent work systems are translated upon their diffusion to a different national business system. There is an enactment through social patterns of interaction in organizations. Organizations are not simply driven to incorporate practices and procedures defined by prevailing rationalized concepts of organizational work. As the case studies show, there is not a standard pattern of accepting alternative work systems. This contrasts isomorphism and convergence arguments (see for example DiMaggio and Powell, 1991) where adopter firms copy a particular work practice that they perceive as best practice. Although there is evidence to suggest that 'path-dependent distinctiveness' of national forms of capitalist organizations still apply (see Ferner, 2000), firms are not as uniform within each capitalist system as is suggested by authors such as Orrù et al (1991).

The study reported here presents multilevel influences on the diffusion process. There are very few multilevel comprehensive studies that focus on both structure *and* process in the diffusion of work systems across nations (exceptions include Maurice et al., 1986; Sorge, 1989, 1996; Child and Loveridge, 1990). For example, Sorge (1996, p. 73) highlights the structure and flow aspects of organizational, human resources, industrial-sectoral, labour market and technical dimensions in the 'reproduction of societal patterns' among Europeans firms. The significance of the present study rests on its efforts to bring together discrete strands of work. The focus is not on social patterns of interaction at the organizational level alone.

The case study findings contribute to the minority of studies that have addressed the sectoral characteristics of nations (such as Porter, 1990) and technological innovation (such as Pavitt, 1984). The focus is on the role of social institutions in explaining the dynamics of work systems diffusion. Hence, there is an attempt to highlight the *structural influences* on diffusion as well as the *process* of internalizing work systems within organizations. The focus on the *internalization* process eliminates a static orientation that is commonly observed in innovation research that focuses on *implementation* alone (Wolfe, 1994). In other words, the study considers both technical and social arrangements (Sorge, 1989). The structural and technological characteristics are not taken as the primary determinants of the diffusion of knowledge-driven work systems. The study highlights the fact that the nature of work systems (that is, tacit cultural and control-related and explicit structural and technological features) can influence the diffusion process.

There is a move here away from a deterministic perspective on diffusion towards an investigation of the nature of characteristics that are likely to influence diffusion processes and how the influences interact. The unit of analysis is the diffusion process itself. Hence, the study incorporates process-oriented research that involves cross-sectional description of the conditions that influence the implementation and internalization process. This research differs from the work of researchers in the innovation processes literature, such as Norton and Bass (1987) and Attewell (1992), by extending its scope beyond the influence of organizational and work systems characteristics on the extent of work systems diffusion to include the influence of the national and local institutional characteristics.

The institutional gap between the source and the adopter firm observed in this study can influence the pattern of diffusion to Japanese affiliate firms in other business systems. For example, employment stability, the acquisition of skills through heavy investments in training, and long-term strategic planning characteristic of the German business system might be expected to present less of a challenge to the diffusion of Japanese work systems. However, there are also institutional constraints to such transfer within the German system, not least the ability of unions and powerful works councils to influence work practice innovation. For example, Dore (2000) argues that in the 1990s, despite the growing pressures on German firms to cut costs, there was strong resistance from German unions both to 'teamwork', which would blur the connection between individual effort and reward, and to any unpaid worker contribution, through mechanisms such as 'quality circles', to the firm's prosperity (see also Streeck, 1997).

3.   PRACTICAL IMPLICATIONS

General Implications for Management

As was pointed out in Chapter One, the diffusion of work systems can be regarded as a critical management issue, for it is closely associated with competitive strength. The implementation and internalization of work systems has implications for the quality and productivity of the output produced. The quality and productivity concerns require well thought-out and planned human resource practices that can allow tacit knowledge of employees to develop and interact with the firm. Firms that are familiar with the knowledge-driven nature of their work systems can be expected to invest in the people they hire and train to impart both the techniques and philosophies of continuous improvement schemes to them. For example, high employee turnover, which is seen as a problem in sustaining the Japanese training system in UK adopter firms, suggests a need to adopt a long-term perspective to developing employees. It is argued that the largest return on investment in training can be recovered only over a long-term relationship (Cutcher-Gershenfeld et al., 1998). Hence, it is important to allow time to build sustained interdependent relationships and to invest in social contracts. This also means emphasizing tacit as well as explicit practices in continuous improvement to create an environment that is a nexus for learning and creativity.

The case study findings show that the sense-making process of employees has a role to play in the effective implementation of alternative work systems. A long-term perspective and hands-on approach to management may build the employee commitment necessary in the implementation of alternative work systems. It is also advantageous to be sensitive to the local institutional characteristics or social attributes pertaining to each location site in nurturing and recreating firm-specific skills across national boundaries. As Fruin (1997) shows, emulation and adaptation rather than imitation tend to work. The interpretation of employment practices such as employment security, seniority and job definition, job designs, staffing and skilling deployments has implications for the effective implementation of continuous improvement schemes. Given that 'workplace-centred, co-operative human resource strategies are at the heart of Japan's industrial success and several features of this approach are distinctive' (Fruin, 1997, p. 212), it is important to recognize and reflect the understanding of continuous improvement as it is held at the source company. Having a comprehensive view of the practices to be diffused can be helpful in facilitating the implementation and internalization of work systems within the firm. In other words, structural, cultural, control-related and technological practices need to be diffused in combination for an integrated understanding of a source firm's work systems. This has implications for generating innovations that provide opportunities for growth. It is the process of sense-making and knowledge creation, not just results, that drives continuous improvement.

This study raises managerial awareness of the implementation of corporate policies at different organizations. The intention has been to highlight the inner workings and tensions within affiliate firms of multinational corporations through a multilevel study that systematically compares workers' and managers' views through interviews and participant observation. The interest in the process of internalizing work systems can reveal insights into the dynamics between forces of convergence and divergence in the organization of work, as well as in managerial forms and institutions of industrial relations. Management can consider the fit between institutional environments and strategic analyses prior to investments in overseas markets to reduce the risk of failure of start-up operations or international alliances.

Implications for Firms in the Automotive Sector

Apart from the general implications for management addressed in the previous section, issues applicable to the current fundamental shifts in the UK and Japanese institutional environments can be discussed.

By now, firms in the automotive sector are well aware of the changes in work systems that have swept through those vehicle manufacturers of the 'West' which have sought to emulate their Japanese competitors. 'In Europe and in the USA, that process of change has been given added impetus by the arrival of Japanese transplant assembly plants and a growing R&D presence, together with the arrival of Japanese components suppliers' (GEAC, 1999). The automotive sector has been continually transforming in the way in which business is carried out, with 'Western' vehicle manufacturers emulating the new lean manufacturing and supply practices of the Japanese component suppliers and car manufacturers. This transformation tends to blur the boundaries of national business systems. The accelerating internalization of Japanese work systems sets the rules of competition in the UK automotive sector in that firms in this sector are urged to invest heavily in the development of knowledge and sufficient production capacity to avoid slipping into the role of marginal players with unfavourable prospects in the future.

With respect to rapid industry-wide restructuring, the UK automotive sector seems to have an advantage over its Japanese counterpart. In comparison to the business system of Japan, the compartmentalized system of the UK is weakly institutionalized in terms of the nature of its obligational ties (see Chapter Two). Hence, competences of firms located in compartmentalized systems can be regarded as more mobile across borders.[1] For example, Ferner (2000, p. 32) argues that 'knowledge stored in codified form is relatively transparent and accessible and, therefore, is readily transferable between business systems.' He regards the business knowledge and organizational capabilities of US firms as explicit and codified, in comparison with those of Japanese firms, allowing them to be reproduced in foreign settings. It is argued that weak obligational ties allow compartmentalized systems to be more receptive to alternative work practices and competences (see Whitley, 1999c). Firms in compartmentalized systems have the relevant institutional make-up to capitalize on the knowledge of others, as they are likely to be more externally oriented to accommodate fragmented training systems, discourage collaboration and emphasize explicit knowledge than those in highly coordinated business systems.

The Japanese business system has also witnessed an ongoing restructuring process since the early 1990s. However, this change is more commonly observed in the financial than in the manufacturing sector. For example, with the liberalization of the Japanese financial market, Japanese company analysts' roles and tasks have changed to include responsibility for primary as well as secondary market transactions (Kubo and Saka, 2002). The traditional Japanese management system, based on lifetime employment and seniority-based salary system (Sako and Sato, 1997), faces challenges with the 'Westernization' of the financial industry (Hamada and Horiuchi, 1999). It should be noted that the Japanese financial industry interacts more readily with the 'Western' financial industry. Hence, it is influenced to a greater degree than, for instance, the Japanese automotive or the electronics industry.

The interactions of Japanese firms with generally Anglo-Saxon firms in home or international markets appear to have an impact on the broader institutional context, particularly the labour market in Japan (Koike, 1993). Although there is a shift away from traditional, centralized bureaucracies to greater inter-firm collaborations, this is not strongly felt across all institutions in Japan. The threat of external competition has only recently been perceived as a problem. The blurring of institutional boundaries of the Japanese business system is much slower than that observed in the UK. It is far more difficult to initiate change in institutions that have grown strong roots in distinct cultures and social processes. For example, the egalitarianism embedded in Japanese society tends to deprive researchers and scholars of the economic incentives to pursue creative and innovative studies (Hirao, 2001). The national system of industrial relations in Japan tends to limit receptivity to alternative work systems. Given the strong embeddedness in networks of mutual obligations and commitment, firms in the Japanese business system implement incremental, continuous change. This is well illustrated by the slow transformation of the Japanese economy since the burst of the bubble in the early 1990s (see for example Dirks et al., 2000).

Implications for Government Policy

The case study findings reflect the role of government in the automotive sector in the diffusion of alternative work systems to the UK.

The UK government has a drive to pursue a policy of extending 'manufacturing excellence' in every part of the UK. The diffusion of work systems in the spread of such 'excellence' is seen as vital to the country's ability to compete in the future and to create wealth through productivity improvements across the whole economy. This is no wonder given that manufacturing 'accounts for about a fifth of our [the UK's] national income with almost £150 billion of output per year' (Byers, 2001). Manufacturing processes are undergoing transformation as a result of increasing competition from newly industrializing countries, improvements in productivity, and generally as a consequence of automation and new technology. The role of government is to help manage this change in the manufacturing sector. It could equip people to create conditions that enable individuals to meet the challenges. In other words, the government can invest in skills to make the most of 'new' work systems to raise innovation in every region as well as provide a platform for economic stability with low inflation and steady growth.

The case study findings provide a partial answer to the following government policy-related question: 'What is the impact of foreign investment on the UK labour relations and management systems?' Although commitment to improving the UK's manufacturing base has improved in terms of an increase in inward investment (some £6–8 billion in 2000) in the automotive sector in general, resources are specifically allotted to regions that are most affected by industrial restructuring and most dependent on the manufacturing industry (Byers, 2001). This means that regions popular for tourism, such as that of Teniki UK, are not given the opportunity to benefit from the activities of industry forum adaptation programmes, 'best practices' in production and supply chain management or the activities of Manufacturing Excellence Centres. An increase in the skills level in regions that are less dependent on manufacturing may facilitate the adoption of manufacturing philosophies and techniques in coping with shifting demands in the industry and encourage a long-term outlook on sustaining expected quality, cost and delivery outcomes. Government initiatives to increase the skills level of the workforce in the location area of Teniki UK may (in combination with the appropriate managerial strategies) create the environment necessary for the implementation and internalization of knowledge-driven work systems. For instance, the UK government's investment in Wales to create a 'premier' location, infrastructure and cost base is seen as having yielded some of the following key benefits: commitment to quality; loyal skilled workforce; low unit labour costs and high productivity; vibrant economy geared for significant growth; facilities and infrastructure geared to suit the needs of international businesses, and administration that is supportive and welcoming (Invest.UK, 2000).

The government could be sensitive to the impact of institutional (local as well as national) characteristics on the effective running of knowledge-driven Japanese work systems at the firm level in the UK for the following reasons: first, the manufacturing sector is regarded as vital to the country's ability to compete globally (Byers, 2001); and second, the manufacturing sector is seen as running second only to the service sector in recent years in terms of output and employment growth (Invest.UK, 2000).

Limitations of the Study

The research design and conceptual framework are not without their limitations. The generalization of findings to other sectors of manufacturing or to the service sector should be approached with caution. If the meanings attached to the use of Japanese work systems can vary across sites within the same sector, then differences can be expected between different manufacturing sectors. However, the salient organizational characteristics identified in the study as explanatory factors (particularly the interplay of actors, resources and the nature of diffused practices) may be expected to have wider applicability.

An attempt is made in this study to be comprehensive with regard to the levels of investigation and nature of diffused practices. This broad coverage may at times have been more prevailing than the need to provide an in-depth analysis within a particular level of investigation and/or form of practice. For example, the study has not allowed the researcher to investigate macro-level processes in detail. Rather, the diffusion of work systems is systematically analysed at the local institutional and organizational levels within a specific sector. A cross-national comparison of paired companies in Japan and the UK has not been carried out owing to the limited scope of the study.[2] Hence, it has not been ascertained in great detail how key national social institutions – the state, financial system, public training system, legal system, authority relations and union strength listed in Chapter One – directly or indirectly influence the local institutional characteristics or the actions of management. Future research is needed to detail the nature of the influence of national institutional characteristics on the diffusion of work systems within the two countries. As this study stands, the impact of national social institutions is discussed at a theoretical level.

Another limitation of this study is that the range of key characteristics that are identified as having an impact on the diffusion of alternative work systems is not all-encompassing. Future research that is ethnographic in nature can identify other relevant characteristics that can explain the same outcome. Nonetheless, influential characteristics are identified here through a multilevel analysis. Insights into the diffusion of work systems are provided through research that combines micro- and macro-level analyses. Hence, it has been possible to identify organizational characteristics that channel and constrain adopters in putting into practice and accepting knowledge-driven work systems. A process dimension to investigating the diffusion of work systems, highlighting the role of managers and workers in the process, has been added to the study. Moreover, possible mutual influences between various local institutional and organizational characteristics have been suggested wherever possible. For instance, the nature of Japanese involvement in the activities of the adopter firms was linked to the organizational characteristic of company age. In addition, this research lent itself to the 'method of difference' in a comparative case study. Two of the companies (Teniki UK and Rover) were of similar local institutional environment, whilst the remaining company (Nissera UK) had a dissimilar local institutional setting. This research design provided stronger empirical evidence about the influence of local institutional characteristics on the diffusion of Japanese knowledge-driven work systems.

This study is limited to analysing the *combined* influence of characteristics at multiple levels. Furthermore, salient characteristics that are likely to influence the degree of implementation alone have not been distinguished from those that are likely to have an impact on the degree of internalization. Rather, it has been assumed that a higher level of implementation of a particular practice is associated with a higher level of internalization of that practice (see Section Two in Chapter One).

It should also be noted that although, at the organizational level, salient tacit elements of continuous improvement schemes such as the level of worker commitment have been highlighted in this study, a particular sequence and priorities that can guide the process of putting alternative work systems into practice is not reported. Instead, the importance of managing the interdependence between tacit (that is, largely the intangible) and explicit (that is, largely the tangible) components of continuous improvements schemes in diffusion efforts is highlighted.

4.   A FUTURE RESEARCH AGENDA

The case study findings show pointers to the future as follows:

First of all, the impact of nationally distinct institutions on the implementation and internalization of alternative work systems can be examined in the UK *and* Japan. The findings reveal that further research is needed into testing the full presence of favourable and unfavourable key institutional and organizational characteristics through a direct comparison of diffusion processes in Japan and the UK. Research into more cohesive institutional environments than those investigated here requires a cross-national study of firms that are highly reflective of their national business system, rather than research based on MNCs. For example, Ferner (2000) contends that host systems just as much as parent systems are prone to institutional heterogeneity. In other words, national business systems may be characterized by heterogeneous sub-systems, reflected in regional or sectoral differences.

Stronger empirical evidence can be provided with regard to the impact of the institutional variation between the structural and cultural legacies of 'highly coordinated' systems and those of 'compartmentalized' systems by expanding the empirical base to include the US business system, which is also classified as a 'compartmentalized' system (Whitley, 1999b). Furthermore, the conceptual framework can be expanded to test for the degree of and patterns in learning by source firms. Although there has been a mention of the extent to which Teniki, Nissera and Honda were willing to learn from their affiliate firms, this has not been discussed in detail here. Future research can investigate the diffusion of work systems from UK adopter firms to Japanese source firms. This would be highly relevant in the light of the current debates on the inefficiency of the Japanese management system. The sectoral differences in patterns of learning can be explored. Functions that are undergoing transformation in highly coordinated systems and the impact of this transformation on performance outcomes can be systematically reported. For instance, according to Westney (1993, p. 65), Japanese firms may 'try to learn from and adapt some of the adjustments to their organizational patterns not only for their future plants in Europe but for their Japanese plants as well, as the Japanese institutional environment changes over time'.[3]

The investigation of the diffusion of organizational practices can be extended to include the impact of these practices on stakeholder relations. For example, in the case of the automotive sector, one can examine how the Japanese cultivate close supplier linkages. Do the Japanese want to reinforce and institutionalize the production organization of the branch plant? The Rover–Honda collaboration site exemplifies the shift towards enhanced supplier relations, whereby the adopter firm uses suppliers as guest engineers on its site in a partnership-style working relationship. If there is an intention to reinforce the production organization, how is this affected by recent advances in IT, global procurement, increased outsourcing and change to the supply chain that are currently influencing the shape of the automotive sector? How is the development of firm-specific skills influenced by these recent trends?

Secondly, the research findings can be linked to financial indicators so as to demonstrate how the diffusion of knowledge-driven work systems in internationalization efforts relates to MNCs' performance in such respects as profitability and growth. For example, it became apparent during data collection in the two subsidiary firms that Japanese management was increasingly reluctant to diffuse know-how, as the concerned firms displayed weak financial performance and limited ability to develop their own knowledge base. The link to financial indicators would allow for a stepwise anchoring and weighing of the more qualitative field study findings. A survey could complement qualitative case study research.

Thirdly, further research could be conducted to provide evidence of the impact of institutional variation across sectors within the same and/or different national business systems. For example, the financial services sector can be included to widen the empirical base. The research could aim to answer the following question: are practices of firms in the financial sector such as task specialization, structures for communicating and adding value to information and personnel development programmes more diffusable than the core practices of firms in the automotive manufacturing sector? Child and Loveridge (1990, p. 12) demonstrate that there are variations in choice, dialogue, power and process across banking, health care and retailing sectors in Belgium, Hungary, Italy, Sweden, the United Kingdom and Germany, China, Poland and Yugoslavia 'arising from influences specific to the historical, cultural, social and economic context as well as from a degree of indeterminacy in the process of deciding on a given technological innovation'. They argue for multiple paths to introduction of information technology (IT). They show that the process of discussing and negotiating results in different applications of the same microelectronic-based technology in different sectors and countries. The institutional and legal framework for decision-making and values that impinge upon authority, control, solidarity and job definition are shown to be among the key influences.

Similarly, even though this research takes into account the nature of the relationship between the Japanese source and the UK adopter firms in the diffusion of work systems, it does not include different ownership structures such as state-owned and private firms or unionized and non-unionized firms. The sample of firms investigated can be enlarged depending on the dominance of a particular ownership structure in the institutional setting of interest.

Fourthly, the case study findings show that Japanese expatriates act as crucial agents in the diffusion of work systems. Similarly, Sharpe et al.'s (2000) findings show that expatriate managers play a central role in creating networks, coordinating and mediating expectations and realities or in 'translating' understandings between local managers and members at the Japanese headquarters. Future research can provide greater detail of information on their role in skills and trust formation in partnerships and the implications of their diffusion efforts across international collaborations for building firm-specific competences. Such research can focus, for example, on how and under what circumstances Japanese expatriates translate their experiences in a particular business system to suit the local needs in other institutional environments.

Fifthly, actors' process of translating alternative work systems can be studied in more detail. For example, one can examine how tacit knowledge is converted into explicit knowledge (and vice versa) in the context of an engineering design. As Ferguson (1997, p. 58) contends, 'The machines and structures designed by engineers could not be built if sensual knowledge in shop and field did not range far beyond its visual component.' In other words, sensual non-verbal knowledge and subtle acts of knowledge, that is the knowledge and skills of workers, are crucial to engineering design. An empirical investigation can provide insights into how knowledge of current practice and products and a growing base of first-hand knowledge and insights gained through critical field observation of engineering projects and industrial plants yield creative designs. Such research on processes conducive to the externalization of knowledge can be linked to the notion of creativity, and this may vary across nations (see for example Appleyard, 1996). In the 1950s, this notion became a fad that swept through the US engineering schools. The interest in a creativity craze waned a decade later (Ferguson, 1997). However, the notion of creativity is as important today as it was in the 1950s. The training systems that encourage the use of intuition and non-verbal thought, rather than single-answer problems, may be more conducive to the production of creative designs.[4] One can consider the home country effect in one's investigation of such training systems. Research does hint that knowledge creation processes in different sectors such as science, technology and law may differ, for example, in terms of the reliance on explicit knowledge as in documentation (see for example Robertson, 1999).

Lastly, it was suggested in this study that the organizational level could have a 'trickling-up' impact on the regional and national levels. This impact could be observed on the nature of industrial relations in the location areas of the adopter firms. The UK institutional environment is in the process of transforming with the growth in Japanese FDI and emulation of Japanese manufacturing processes. The impact of this transformation on public training systems, the role of the state, the financial system, the legal system, authority relations and union strength can be explored through future research. This can be a means of avoiding environmental determinism that can be ascribed to neo-institutional theory.

5. SUMMARY

A comparison of the degree to which work systems are implemented and internalized in three affiliate firms of Japanese MNCs in the UK automotive sector has highlighted variation in diffusion. The Japanese source company's practices, embedded in highly coordinated systems, are found to be challenged at the national and organizational levels by a conflicting set of structural and cultural legacies and an emphasis on explicit practices embedded in compartmentalized systems. The Teniki UK site displays a setting in which predominantly unfavourable institutional and organizational characteristics contribute to a low degree of implemention and internalization. By contrast, Nissera UK and Rover–Honda collaboration sites exhibit a setting in which predominantly favourable institutional and organizational characteristics contribute to a relatively high degree of implementation and internalization of work systems. At the national level, in a similar way to Teniki UK, Nissera UK and the Rover–Honda collaboration are embedded in a business system that discourages an emphasis on tacit knowledge, team culture, sense of discipline, cooperation and knowledge-sharing. Nevertheless, a combination of favourable local institutional and organizational characteristics, including supportive managerial initiatives and worker response, has a positive impact on the diffusion of work systems to Nissera UK and Rover.

The case study findings indicate that, despite the trend towards globalization, there is in effect a diversity in the adoption of alternative work systems that are strongly embedded in distinct forms of business systems by adopter firms which are embedded, comparatively, in weakly institutionalized settings. The source company's 'exemplary' practices are translated as they are imitated. The institutional gap between the source and the adopter firm forms a space for translating standardized models. In line with Westney's (1987) argument, one innovates as one imitates, that is models change as they spread (see Sevón, 1996). This issue has implications for management and the government, in particular, owing to the association of work systems diffusion with competitive strength. Nevertheless, there is still a large uninvestigated field of research with regard to institutional compatibility in the area of work systems diffusion, especially in demonstrating the impact of the diffusion process on an MNC's financial performance. This would provide for more practical solutions to management.

NOTES

1. However, mobile competences are not necessarily associated with effective and efficient systems of production. For example, the fact that firms in compartmentalized systems may not have major operations overseas is not dependent on the mobility of competences alone. Such firms' systems may not be seen as efficient and effective.
2. Under a different research design, it would have been possible to conduct a comparative study of the diffusion of work systems in the UK and the Japanese contexts.

3. These changes can include shortage of skilled labour, which may necessitate greater employment of women and the move to greater flexibility of rewards (Westney, 1993).
4. The use of intuition and non-verbal thought refers to the ability to think pictorially, not just mathematically (see Ferguson, 1997).

Appendices

APPENDIX I   KEY EVENTS IN THE ROVER–HONDA RELATIONSHIP

Table A.1   Key events in the Rover–Honda relationship

Date	Event
September 1978	First contact in Tokyo
October 1978	Working meeting in San Francisco
April 1979	First joint press release
December 1979	Triumph Acclaim agreement signed
1981	Triumph Acclaim launched
1982	Rover 800/Honda Legand project commenced
1984	Rover 200 launched (replaced Triumph Acclaim)
1985	R8/YY Project commenced (Second generation Rover 200/400, Honda Concerto)
1986	Rover 800 launch, Rover build subcontract Legend for Honda, Rover build subcontract Ballade for Honda
1987	Honda build subcontract Rover 800 in Japan
1989	Rover 200/Concerto launch, Honda open UK factory at Swindon (HUM), HUM supplies power units for Rover 200/Concerto
1990	20% cross shareholding between Rover and HUM, Rover 600/Accord project commenced
1991	Second generation Rover 400/Civic commenced
1992	HUM-built Accord launched
1993	Rover 600 launched, Crossroad launched
1994	BMW purchase Rover Group, HUM-built Civic launched
1995	Rover 400 launched

Source: Liaison Office, Rover Group

APPENDIX II   LIST OF INTERVIEWEES

Table A.2   List of interviewees at Teniki UK

Site		Participants	Interview date
(Teniki UK) (A visit per month; poor financial circumstances discouraged visits from April 1999 to June 1999)	1	(British) MD	21 August 1998 and 15 February 1999
	2	(Japanese) Senior Advisor in Sales and Marketing	17 December 1998
	3	(Japanese) Technical Advisor in Design	17 December 1998
	4	(British) Quality Engineer	17 December 1998
	5	(British) Product Engineer	17 December 1998
	6	(British) Account Manager	15 February 1999
	7	(British) Personnel and Training Manager	15 February 1999
	8	(British) Canister Supervisor	15 February 1999
	9	(British) Design Manager	16 March 1999
	10	(British) Product Engineer	16 March 1999
	11	(Japanese) Senior Advisor in Engineering	16 March 1999
	12	(Japanese) Senior Advisor in Engineering	18 January 2000
	13	(British) Team Coach in Carbon Canister	28 July 1999
Work experience as an operator	14	(British) Team Coach in Air Element	26–29 July 1999
	15	(British) Quality Auditor	28 July 1999
	16	(British) Personnel and Training Assistant	29 July 1999
	17	(British) Team Coach in Air Element	18 January 2000
	18	(British) Operations Manager	18 January 2000
Teniki Ltd. (interviews at the parent company in Japan)	19	(Japanese) Deputy GM, International Operations Department	7 April 2000
	20	(Japanese) Senior Manager, Development Division	7 April 2000

Table A.3   List of interviewees at Nissera UK

Site		Participants	Interview date
(Nissera UK)	1	(British) Account Manager	30 April 1999
Work experience	2	(British) Senior Team Leader in	14 June 1999
as an operator		Assembly	
14–17 June 1999	3	(British) Senior Team Leader in	14 June 1999
		Assembly	
Worked in Cell1	4	(British) Team Leader in Assembly	14 June 1999
and Cell2		(in charge of Cell1 and Cell4)	
	5	(British) Team Leader in Assembly	14 June 1999
		(Cell2 and S1)	
Worked in Cell3	6	(British) Team Leader in Assembly	15 June 1999
and Cell4		(Cell3 and Cell7)	
Worked in Cell5	7	(British) Team Leader in Assembly	16 June 1999
and Cell7		(Cell5 and Cell8)	
Worked in	8	(British) Team Leader	17 June 1999
Cell8, S1	9	(British Moulding Manager	17 June 1999
	10	(British) Purchasing and Production	30 July 1999
		Control Manager	
	11	(British) Production Manager	30 July 1999
	12	(British) Group Leader in Customer	30 July 1999
		Quality	
	13	(British) Management Accounts	30 July 1999
		Manager	
	14	(Japanese) Quality Director	13 September 1999
Nissera Ltd.	15	(Japanese) Deputy Manager, General	12 April 2000
(interviews at		Affairs Department	
the parent	16	(Japanese) Manager in Production	13 April 2000
company in		Department 1	
Japan)	17	(Japanese) Manager in Quality	13 April 2000
		Assurance Supervision Department	
	18	(Japanese) Manager in Corporate	14 April 2000
		Finance Department	
	19	(Japanese) Manager in Electronics	· 14 April 2000
		Engineering Department 1	
	20	(Japanese) Manager in Corporate	14 April 2000
		Planning and Control Department	

*Table A.4   List of interviewees at Rover Group and Honda Motor Co.
Rover 200/Honda Concerto (R8/YY) project*

Site		Participants		Interview date
Rover Group	1	(British) Ex-director of Honda Collaboration		21 January 1999
	2	(British) Senior Purchasing Manager of Rover Group Projects		16 February 1999
	3	(British) Principal Electrical Engineer	A	24 February 1999
	4	(British) Chief Predevelopment Electrical Engineer		11 March 1999
	5	(British) Chief Advanced Power Train Engineer		2 April 1999
	6	(British) Principal Electrical Engineer	B	9 April 1999
	7	(British) Principal Electrical Engineer	C	13 April 1999
	8	(British) General Manager of Honda Collaboration		15 April 1999
	9	(British) Electrical Team Leader	D	16 April and 21 May 1999
	10	(British) Logistics Operations Manager		23 April 1999
	11	(British) Electrical Group Leader	E	7 May 1999
	12	(British) Principal Electrical Engineer	F	7 May and 21 June 1999
	13	(British) Principal Systems Engineer on Rover 800	G	10 May 1999
	14	(British) Principal Electrical Engineer	H	12 May 1999
	15	(British) Chief Designer		14 May 1999
	16	(British) Principal Electrical Engineer	I	24 May and 21 June 1999
	17	(British) Team Leader	J	27 May 1999
	18	(British) Principal Electrical Engineer	K	2 June 1999
	19	(British) Design Director		22 June 1999
	20	(British) Principal Mechanical Engineer	L	22 June 1999
	21	(British) Design and Development Engineer		23 June 1999
	22	(British) Project Engineer on Central Components		21 July 1999
	23	(British) Senior Management in Manufacturing Integration (current)		25 August, 9 September and 6 October 1999
Honda Motor Co. Ltd.	24	(Japanese) Ex-director of Rover Collaboration at Honda Motor Europe (HME)		17 April 1999 (by e-mail) and 30 March 2000 (in Japan)

Table A.4 (continued)

Site		Participants		Interview date
	25	(Japanese) Manager at Rover Liaison Office of Honda Motor Europe		29 April 1999
	26	(British) Purchasing Divisional Manager, Honda UK Manufacturing (HUM)		22 September 1999
	27	(Japanese) Executive VP of Honda R&D Europe		29 March 2000
	28	(Japanese) Principal Engineer (currently Assistant Chief Engineer)	A H	29 March 2000
	29	(Japanese) Principal Engineer (currently Assistant Chief Engineer)	B H	29 March 2000
	30	(Japanese) Principal Engineer (currently Assistant Chief Engineer)	C H	29 March 2000
	31	(Japanese) Project member on the XX project (currently Production Planning Manager)		3 and 4 April 2000
	32	(Japanese) Project Manager (currently MD of Honda Foundation)		5 April 2000
	33	(Japanese) Project Leader (currently MD of Car Development at Nissera Ltd.)		13 April 2000

APPENDIX III   THE INTERVIEW PROTOCOL

The research participants were familiar with the research objectives and the background of the researcher prior to the scheduled meetings. General information on the name, position and roles and responsibilities of the participants, interview dates and times, as well as the name of the organization, were recorded at each sampled firm.

Name of the organization:
Name of the participant:
Position of the participant:
Date of the interview:
Start and end time of the interview:
Nature of the job (i.e. roles and responsibilities):

List of Interview Questions

I.   Institutional level
Institutional level questions were directed to local development agencies such as the Economic Development and Tourism Units and the District and Borough Councils. Secondary sources of information such as newspaper articles were also used. Questions (which were in general the same for all three sampled firms) centred on the following issues:

1.   Age and skill level of the labour force
2.   Employment by sector as an indicator of tradition of manufacturing
3.   Level of unemployment in the area
4.   Number of overseas companies in the region
5.   Government initiative for investment (i.e. inward investment)
6.   Level of industrial dispute

Questions Directed to Teniki UK and Nissera UK

II.   Organizational level
1.   What was the organization like before the acquisition by Teniki?
2.   With what purpose was the subsidiary established?
3.   How is the subsidiary financed?
4.   Would you say that you have 'Japanized'?
    4.1   What is the role of technology in this process?
5.   How different is managing a brownfield site from that of a greenfield site?
6.   Have there been structural changes?

7. What is the role of the parent company in the subsidiary firm's operations?
    7.1 What is the nature of the relationship with the parent company?
    7.2 How successful is it?
8. What kind of cultural and managerial differences between the subsidiary and the parent firm do you perceive?
    8.1 How are these managed?
9. Which practices* of the parent firm are transferred* to the subsidiary?
10. Do you feel that the working relationship between the parent company and subsidiary firm could be better?
    10.1 What could be done differently to improve it?
11. What is the parent company learning from its subsidiary?
    11.1 What mechanisms are there for sharing ideas?
12. How are parent company's practices, such as continuous improvement activities, transferred to the subsidiary firm?
    12.1 Is there an emphasis on documentation?
13. How did the Japanese train senior managers?
14. What are the barriers preventing the adoption of Japanese practices at the subsidiary firm?
15. Is quality assessment effectively implemented at the subsidiary firm?
16. Is there a different level of resistance to different types of transferred practices?
17. Which factors* make it easier for the employees at the subsidiary firm to accept* the parent company's practices?
18. Which practices could not be successfully implemented at the subsidiary firm?
    18.1 Why?
19. What implications has the introduction of Japanese practices had for the subsidiary firm's performance?

> * The terms 'transfer', 'practices', 'factors' and 'accept' were used instead of 'diffusion', 'work systems', 'characteristics' and 'internalize' in the interviews for ease of communication with practitioners. Effort was made to avoid the use of academic terms.

Questions Directed to the Rover Group and Honda Motor Co. Ltd.

II. Organizational level

1. What was the nature of your relationship with Honda [Rover]?
    1.1 How successful was it?
    1.2 Why?

2. Was there a clear division of responsibility between Honda and Rover?
3. Which Honda practices were transferred to Rover in general?
4. How did the local practice/custom limit the extent to which Honda ideas were accepted at Rover in general?
   4.1 Was there a different level of resistance to different types of practices?
5. Which practices could not be successfully implemented at Rover?
   5.1 Why?
6. Which practices disappeared over time at Rover?
   6.1 Why?
7. What kind of cultural and managerial differences between Rover and Honda did you perceive?
   7.1 How were these managed?
8. What did Honda learn from Rover? What did Rover learn from Honda?
9. Which Honda practices were transferred specifically to the collaborative project you were involved in?
   9.1 Did you make use of these practices in the joint project?
   9.2 How were these practices transferred?
   9.3 Was there an emphasis on documentation?
10. Which factors helped in the transfer process?
11. Which factors made it difficult to transfer practices?
12. How did the local practice/custom limit the extent to which Honda ideas were accepted at Rover specifically at the joint project level?
    12.1 Was there a different level of resistance to different types of practices?
13. In your joint development of the Rover 200/Honda Concerto, what mechanisms were there for sharing ideas?
14. Would currently available knowledge databases on the intranet have contributed to effective working relations if they were available at the time of the Rover 200/Honda Concerto project?
15. Do you feel that the working relationship between Rover and Honda engineers could have been better on the Rover 200/Honda Concerto project?
    15.1 What could have been done differently to improve it?
16. What did you learn from Rover at a project and an individual level?
    16.1 How would you implement what you learnt on the Rover 200/Honda Concerto project on a joint project of a similar nature with another British [Japanese] firm?

APPENDIX IV   SALES AND PROFIT TRENDS BETWEEN 1993 AND 1999 AT NISSERA UK

Table A.5   Sales and profit trends between 1993 and 1999 at Nissera UK

Fiscal year	Sales (£)	Profits (%)
1993	25,259,000	−0.2
1994	28,891,000	−41.7
1995	34,487,000	−268.3
1996	42,251,000	−241.3
1997	52,984,000	5.1
1998	59,936,000	45.4
1999	50,750,000	100.0

N.B. Profits are calculated in comparison to the figure in 1999

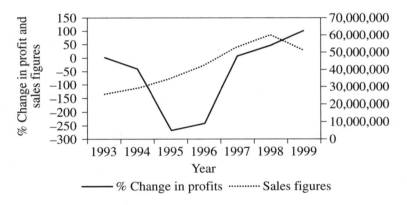

Source: General Affairs Department, Nissera

Figure A.1   Sales and profit trends between 1993 and 1999 at Nissera UK

APPENDIX V   HONDA MOTOR COMPANY'S
COMMUNICATION NETWORK

A data link is not available in Honda's 50-50 collaborations. Rather, there is heavy emphasis on people transfer.

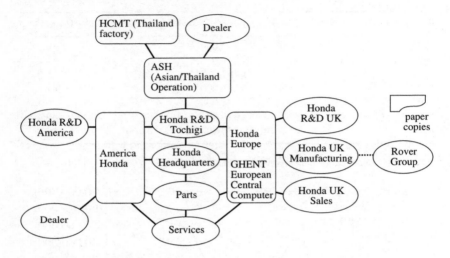

Source: Interview with Japanese project member on the XX at Honda Motor Co. Ltd.
(3 April 2000)

Figure A.2   Honda Motor Company's communication network

APPENDIX VI   THE BENEFIT SCALE

The vertical axis indicates Rover-perceived benefit gained from the relationship with Honda over time.

   In the early years, from 1981 to 1988, the benefit was in excess of incremental product. From 1988 onwards, in addition to incremental product, Rover claimed to have benefited by 'learning from Honda'.

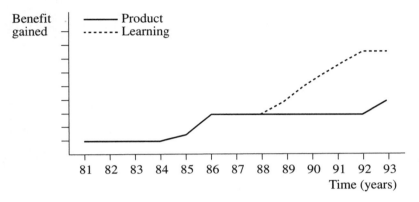

Source: Rover Group, Liaison Office

Figure A.3   The benefit scale

References

Abell, P. (1995), 'The new institutionalism and rational choice theory', in W.R. Scott and S. Christensen (eds), *The Institutional Construction of Organizations*, Thousand Oaks, CA: Sage Publications, pp. 3–14.

Abo, T. (1992), 'Japanese motor vehicle technologies abroad in the 1980s', in D.J. Jeremy (ed.), *The Transfer of International Technology: Europe, Japan and the USA in the Twentieth Century*, Aldershot: Edward Elgar, pp. 167–90.

Abo, T. (1994), *Hybrid Factory: The Japanese Production System in the United States*, Oxford: Oxford University Press.

Abrahamson, E. (1996), 'Management fashion', *Academy of Management Review*, **21**: 254–85.

Abrahamson, E. and L. Rosenkopf (1993), 'Institutional and competitive bandwagons: Using mathematical modelling as a tool to explore innovation diffusion', *Academy of Management Review*, **18** (3): 487–517.

Ackroyd, S., Burrell, G., Hughes, M. and A. Whitaker (1988), 'The Japanization of British industry?', *Industrial Relations Journal*, **19** (1): 1–23.

Adler, P.S. (1992), 'The learning bureaucracy: New United Motor Manufacturing Inc.', *Research in Organizational Behaviour*, **15**: 111–94.

Aiken, M. and J. Hage (1968), 'Organizational interdependence and intra-organizational structure', *American Sociological Review*, **33** (6): 912–30.

Alford, D., Sackett, P. and G. Nelder (2000). 'Mass customization – An automotive perspective', *International Journal of Production Economics*, **65** (1): 99–110.

Altheide, D.L. and J.M. Johnson (1998), 'Criteria for assessing interpretive validity in qualitative research', in N.K. Denzin and Y.S. Lincoln (eds), *Collecting and Interpreting Qualitative Materials*, Thousand Oaks, CA: Sage Publications, pp. 283–312.

Appleyard, M.M. (1996), 'How does knowledge flow? Interfirm patterns in the semiconductor industry', *Strategic Management Journal*, **17**, Winter Special Issue: 137–54.

Araujo, L. (1998), 'Knowing and learning as networking', *Management Learning*, **29** (3): 317–36.

Argyris, C. (1991), 'Teaching smart people how to learn', *Harvard Business Review*, **May–June**: 99–109.

Atkinson, P.A. (1990), *The Ethnographic Imagination: Textual Construc-tions of Reality*, London: Routledge.

Attewell, P. (1992), 'Technology diffusion and organizational learning: the case of business computing', *Organization Science*, **3**: 1–19.

Autocar (1988), 'The fall of the British motor industry', *Autocar*, 11 May: 80–2.

Badaracco, J.L. (1991), *The Knowledge Link: How Firms Compete through Strategic Alliances*, Boston: Harvard Business School Press.

Barker, J.R. (1993), 'Tightening the iron cage: Concertive control in self-managing teams', *Administrative Science Quarterly*, **38** (3): 408–37.

Barney, J.B. (1991), 'Firm resources and sustained competitive advantage', *Journal of Management*, **17**: 99–120.

Beale, D. (1994), *Driven by Nissan? A Critical Guide to the New Management Techniques*, London: Lawrence and Wishart.

Bechhofer, F. and L. Paterson (2000), *Principles of Research Design in the Social Sciences*, London: Routledge.

Bergquist, W., Betwee, J. and D. Meuel (1995), *Building Strategic Relation-ships: How to Extend Your Organization's Reach through Partnerships, Alliances and Joint Ventures*, San Francisco: Jossey-Bass Publishers.

Besser, T.L. (1996), *Team Toyota: Transplanting the Toyota Culture to the Camry Plant in Kentucky*, New York: State University of New York Press.

Best, M.H. (1990), *The New Competition: Institution of Industrial Restructuring*, Cambridge: Polity Press.

Bird, A., Taylor, S. and S. Beechler (1999), 'Organizational learning in Japanese overseas affiliates', in S. Beechler and A. Bird (eds), *Japanese Multinationals Abroad: Individual and Organizational Learning*, New York: Oxford University Press, pp. 235–59.

Blackler, F. (1995), 'Knowledge, knowledge work and organizations: An overview and interpretation', *Organization Studies*, **16** (6): 1021–46.

Blundel, R. and P. Clark (2001), 'Artisanal knowledge and network evolu-tion: A tale of two regional cheesemakers, 1950–2000', Paper presented at the *Managing Knowledge: Conversations and Critiques Conference*, 10–11 April, University of Leicester.

Boisot, M.H. (1995), *Information Space: A Framework for Learning in Organizations, Institutions and Culture*, London: Routledge.

Boyatzis, R.E. (1998), *Transforming Qualitative Information: Thematic Analysis and Code Development*, Thousand Oaks, CA: Sage Publications.

Boyer, R. (1997), 'French statism at the crossroads', in C. Crouch and W. Streeck (eds), *Political Economy of Modern Capitalism: Mapping Convergence and Diversity*, London: Sage Publications, pp. 71–101.

Boyer, R. (1998), 'Hybridization and models of production: Geography, history and theory', in R. Boyer, E. Charron, U. Jürgens and S. Tolliday (eds), *Between Imitation and Innovation: The Transfer and Hybridization of Productive Models in the International Automobile Industry*, Oxford: Oxford University Press, pp. 24–56.

Brannen, M.Y. and J.E. Salk (1999), 'When Japanese and other nationals create something new: A comparative study of negotiated work culture in Germany and the US', in S. Beechler and A. Bird (eds), *Japanese Multinationals Abroad: Individual and Organizational Learning*, New York: Oxford University Press, pp. 33–62.

Brannen, M.Y., Liker, J.K. and W.M. Fruin (1999), 'Recontextualization and factory-to-factory knowledge transfer from Japan to the United States: The case of NSK', in J.K. Liker, W.M. Fruin and P.S. Adler (eds), *Remade in America: Transplanting and Transforming Japanese Management Systems*, New York: Oxford University Press, pp. 117–53.

Braverman, H. (1998), *Labour and Monopoly Capital: The Degradation of Work in the Twentieth Century*, 25th anniversary edition, New York: Monthly Review Press.

Bresman, H., Birkinshaw, J. and R. Noel (1999), 'Knowledge transfer in international acquisitions', *Journal of International Business Studies*, **30** (3): 439–62.

Briggs, P. (1988), 'The Japanese at work: Illusions of the ideal', *Industrial Relations Journal*, **19** (1): 24–30.

British Motor Industry Heritage Trust (1997), *Heritage Motor Centre Catalogue*, Bideford: Bay View Books Limited.

Brunsson, N. (1989), *The Organization of Hypocrisy: Talk, Decisions and Actions in Organizations*, New York: John Wiley and Sons.

Buckley, P.J. and M.J. Carter (1999), 'Managing cross-border complementary knowledge: Conceptual developments in the business process approach to knowledge management in multinational firms', *International Studies of Management and Organization*, **29** (1): 80–104.

Byers, S. (2001), 'Extending manufacturing excellence', *AEEU Seminar*, http://www.dti.gov.uk/ministers/speeches/byers 230101.html, 23 January.

Campbell, J.L., Hollingsworth, J.R. and L.N. Lindberg (1991), *Governance of the American Economy*, Cambridge: Cambridge University Press.

Casper, S. (2000), 'Institutional adaptiveness, technology policy, and the diffusion of new business models: The case of German biotechnology', *Organization Studies*, **21** (5): 887–914.

Casson, M., Loveridge, R. and S. Satwinder (1996), 'Corporate culture in Europe, Asia and North America: Implications for global competition', *Discussion Papers in International Investment and Business Studies*, No. 212, Department of Economics, University of Reading.

Chatman, J. and K. Jehn (1994), 'Assessing the relationship between industry characteristics and organizational culture: How different can you be?', *Academy of Management Journal*, **37**: 522–53.

Chesbrough, H.W. (1998), 'The differing impact of technological change upon incumbent firms: A comparative theory of organizational constraints and national institutional factors', Working Paper, Harvard Business School, Boston.

Chia, R. (2000), 'Metaphysical attitudes and management mindsets: A comparative analysis of East-West strategic orientations, business priorities and practices', Paper presented at the *BAM2000 Conference*, 13–15 September, University of Edinburgh.

Child, J. (1994), *Management in China During the Age of Reform*, Cambridge: Cambridge University Press.

Child, J. and D. Faulkner (1998), *Strategies of Co-operation: Managing Alliances, Networks and Joint Ventures*, Oxford: Oxford University Press.

Child, J. and R. Loveridge (1990), *Information Technology in European Services: Towards a Microelectronic Future*, Oxford: Basil Blackwell Ltd.

Child, J. and S. Rodrigues (1996), 'The role of social identity in the international transfer of knowledge through joint ventures', in S.R. Clegg and G. Palmer (eds), *The Politics of Management Knowledge*, London: Sage Publications, pp. 46–68.

Chung, M.-K. (1998), 'Hyundai tries two industrial models to penetrate global markets', in M. Freyssenet, A. Mair, K. Shimizu and G. Volpato (eds), *One Best Way? Trajectories and Industrial Models of the World's Automobile Producers*, Oxford: Oxford University Press, pp. 154–75.

Cirlot, J.-E. (2001), *Gaudi: An Introduction to his Architecture*, Barcelona: Triangle Postals.

Clark, P. (1987), *Anglo–American Innovation*, New York: Walter de Gruyter.

Clark, P. (2000), *Organizations in Actions: Competition between Contexts*, London: Routledge.

Clark, P. and F. Mueller (1994), 'Organizations and nations: From universalism to institutionalism?', Research Paper, Aston Business School, Aston University, Birmingham.

Clark, P. and S. Newell (1993), 'Societal embedding of production and inventory control systems: American and Japanese influences on adaptive implementation in Britain', *The International Journal of Human Factors in Manufacturing*, **3** (1): 69–81.

Clark, P. and N. Staunton (1989), *Innovation in Technology and Organization*, London: Routledge.

Clark, P., Bennett, D., Burcher, P. and S. Newell (1992), 'The decision-episode framework and computer-aided production management (CAPM)', *International Studies of Management and Organization*, **22** (4): 69–80.

Clark, R. (1979), *The Japanese Company*, New Haven: Yale University Press.

Cole, R.E. (1979), *Work, Mobility and Participation: A Comparative Study of American and Japanese Industry*, Berkeley: University of California Press.

Colombo, M.G. (1998), 'Some introductory reflections', in M.G. Colombo (ed.), *The Changing Boundaries of the Firm: Explaining Evolving Interfirm Relations*, London: Routledge, pp. 1–25.

Crouch, C. and W. Streeck (1997), *Political Economy of Modern Capitalism: Mapping Convergence and Diversity*, London: Sage Publications Ltd.

Cutcher-Gershenfeld, J., Nitta, M., Barret, B.J., Belhedi, N., Chow, S.S., Inaba, T., Ishino, I., Lin, W., Moore, M.L., Mothersell, W.M., Palthe, J., Ramanand, S., Strolle, M.E. and A.C. Wheaton (1998), *Knowledge-Driven Work: Unexpected Lessons from Japanese and United States Work Practices*, Oxford: Oxford University Press.

Czarniawska, B. and G. Sevón (eds) (1996), *Translating Organizational Change*, Berlin: Walter de Gruyter.

Dacin, M.T., Ventresca, M.J. and B.D. Beal (1999), 'The embeddedness of organizations: Dialogue and directions', *Journal of Management*, **25** (3): 317–56.

Dacin, M.T., Goodstein, J. and W.R. Scott (2002), 'Institutional theory and institutional change: Introduction to the special research forum', *Academy of Management Journal*, **45** (1): 45–57.

Danford, A. (1997), 'Labour control and intensification through team-working and kaizen', *Labour Studies Working Papers*, No. 14, Centre for Comparative Labour Studies, University of Warwick, Coventry.

Danford, A. (1998), 'Work organization inside Japanese firms in South Wales: A break from Taylorism', in P. Thompson and C. Warhurst (eds), *Workplaces of the Future*, Basingstoke: Macmillan Business Press Ltd, pp. 40–64.

Davenport, T.H. and L. Prusak (1998), *Working Knowledge: How Organizations Manage What They Know*, Boston: Harvard Business School Press.

Dedoussis, V. (1995), 'Simply a question of cultural barriers? The search for new perspectives in the transfer of Japanese management practices', *Journal of Management Studies*, **32** (6): 731–45.

Delbridge, R. (1995), 'Surviving JIT: Control and resistance in a Japanese transplant', *The Journal of Management Studies*, **32** (6): 803–17.

Delbridge, R. (1998), *Life on the Line in Contemporary Manufacturing: The Workplace Experience of Lean Production and the 'Japanese' Model*, Oxford: Oxford University Press.

Denzin, N.K. and Y.S. Lincoln (1998), *Collecting and Interpreting Qualitative Materials*, London: Sage Publications.

Department of Trade and Industry (1995), *Investing in the Assisted Areas: A Guide to Regional Selective Assistance*, London: Department of Trade and Industry.

Dickens, P. and M. Savage (1988), 'The Japanization of British industry? Instances from a high growth area', *Industrial Relations Journal*, **19** (1): 60–68.

DiMaggio, P.J. and W.W. Powell (1991), 'The iron cage revisited: Institutional isomorphism and collective rationality in organizational fields', in W.W. Powell and P.J. DiMaggio (eds), *The New Institutionalism in Organizational Analysis*, Chicago: The University of Chicago Press, pp. 63–82.

Dirks, D., Hemmert, M., Legewie, J., Meyer-Ohle, H. and F. Waldenberger (2000), 'The Japanese employment system in transition', *International Business Review*, **9** (5): 525–53.

Djelic, M.-L. (1998), *Exporting the American Model: The Post-War Transformation of European Business*, Oxford: Oxford University Press.

Djelic, M.-L. (1999), 'From a typology of neo-institutional arguments to their cross-fertilization', Research Paper, ESSEC, France.

Dobbin, F. (1995), 'The origins of economic principles: Railway entrepreneurs and public policy in 19th-century America', in W.R. Scott and S. Christensen (eds), *The Institutional Construction of Organizations*, Thousand Oaks, CA: Sage Publications, pp. 277–301.

Doorewaard, H., and M. van Bijsterveld (2001), 'The osmosis of ideas: An analysis of the integrated approach to IT management from a translation theory perspective', *Organization*, **8** (1): 55–76.

Dore, R. (1973), *British Factory–Japanese Factory: The Origins of National Diversity in Industrial Relations*, Oxford: University of California Press.

Dore, R. (1997), 'The distinctiveness of Japan', in C. Crouch and W. Streeck (eds), *Political Economy of Modern Capitalism: Mapping Convergence and Diversity*, London: Sage Publications, pp. 19–32.

Dore, R. (2000), *Stock Market Capitalism–Welfare Capitalism: Japan and Germany versus the Anglo-Saxons*, Oxford: Oxford University Press.

Dore, R. and M. Sako (1997), *How the Japanese Learn to Work*, London: Routledge.

Douglas, J.D. (1976), *Investigative Social Research: Individual and Team Field Research*, London: Sage Publications.

Doz, Y. and C.K. Prahalad (1984), 'Patterns of strategic control within multinational corporations', *Journal of International Business Studies*, **15** (2): 55–72.

Dyer, J.H. and K. Nobeoka (2000), 'Creating and managing a

high-performance knowledge-sharing network: The Toyota case', *Strategic Management Journal*, **21**: 345–67.

Eisenhardt, K.M. (1989), 'Building theories from case study research', *Academy of Management Review*, **32**: 543–76.

Elger, T. and C. Smith (1994), *Global Japanization? The Transnational Transformation of the Labour Process*, London: Routledge.

Erramilli, M.K. (1996), 'Nationality and subsidiary ownership patterns in multinational corporations', *Journal of International Business Studies*, Second Quarter, **27**: 225–48.

Faulkner, D. (1995), *International Strategic Alliances: Cooperating to Compete*, London: McGraw-Hill Book Company.

Ferguson, E.S. (1997), *Engineering and the Mind's Eye*, Fourth edition, Cambridge, MA: The MIT Press.

Ferner, A. (2000), 'The embeddedness of US multinational companies in the US business system: Implications for HR/IR', *Occasional Paper Series*, No. 61, Leicester Business School, De Montfort University, Leicester.

Fligstein, N. (1990), *The Transformation of Corporate Control*, Cambridge, MA: Harvard University Press.

Fransman, M. (1994), 'Information, knowledge, vision and theories of the firm', *Industrial and Corporate Change*, **3**: 713–57.

Fruin, W.M. (1997), *Knowledge Works: Managing Intellectual Capital at Toshiba*, Oxford: Oxford University Press.

Fucini, J.J. and S. Fucini (1990), *Working for the Japanese*, New York: Free Press.

Fukuda, K.J. (1987), 'The practice of Japanese-style management in South East Asia', *Journal of General Management*, **13**: 69–81.

GEAC (1999), 'Modular supply in the automotive industry – The next competitive battle: Part 1', http://just-auto.com/features_detail.asp?art=4, 4 January.

George, M. and H. Levie (1984), *Japanese Competition and the British Workforce*, London: Centre for Alternative Industrial and Technological Systems (CAITS).

Gerlach, M. (1992), *Alliance Capitalism*, Berkeley: University of California Press.

Gill, J. and P. Johnson (1991), *Research Methods for Managers*, London: Paul Chapman Publishing Ltd.

Gillham, B. (2000), *Case Study Research Methods*, London: Continuum.

Glaser, B.G. and A.L. Strauss (1967), *The Discovery of Grounded Theory: Strategies for Qualitative Research*, Chicago: Aldine.

Graham, L. (1993), 'Inside a Japanese transplant: A critical perspective', *Work and Occupations*, **20** (2): 147–73.

Grandori, A. and G. Soda (1995), 'Inter-firm networks: Antecedents, mechanisms and forms', *Organization Studies*, **16** (2): 183–214.

Granovetter, M. (1985), 'Economic action and social structure: The problem of embeddedness', *American Journal of Sociology*, **91** (3): 481–510.

Guest, D. (1992), 'Human resource management in the United Kingdom', in B. Towers (ed.), *The Handbook of Human Resource Management*, Oxford: Blackwell Publishers, pp. 3–26.

Håkansson, H. (1986), *Industrial Technological Development: A Network Approach*, London: Croom Helm.

Hall, E.T. (1976), *Beyond Culture*, Garden City, New York: Anchor Press.

Hallier, J. and J. Leopold (2000), 'Managing employment on greenfield sites: Attempts to replicate high commitment practices in the UK and New Zealand', *Industrial Relations Journal*, **31** (3): 177–91.

Hamada, K. and A. Horiuchi (1999), 'The political economy of the financial market', in W.M. Tsutsui (ed.), *Banking in Japan*, 3, London: Routledge, pp. 30–68.

Hamilton, G.G. and N.W. Biggart (1988), 'Market, culture and authority: A comparative analysis of management and organization in the Far East', *American Journal of Sociology*, supplement, **94**: S52–S94.

Hammersley, M. (1992), *What's Wrong with Ethnography? Methodological Explorations*, London: Routledge.

Harzing, A.W.K. (2001), 'Of bears, bumble-bees and spiders: The role of expatriates in controlling foreign subsidiaries', *Journal of World Business*, **36** (4): 366–79.

Hassard, J. (1993), *Sociology and Organization Theory: Positivism, Paradigms and Postmodernity*, Cambridge: Cambridge University Press.

Hayek, F.A. (1945), 'The use of knowledge in society', *American Economic Review*, **35**: 519–30.

Hedlund, G. (1994), 'A model of knowledge management and the N-Form corporation', *Strategic Management Journal*, 15: 73–91.

Hedlund, G. and I. Nonaka (1993), 'Models of knowledge management in the West and Japan', in P. Lorange, B. Chakravarthy, J. Roos and A. Van de Ven (eds), *Implementing Strategic Processes: Change, Learning, and Cooperation*, Oxford: Basil Blackwell, pp. 117–44.

Herrigal, G. (1996), *Industrial Constructions: The Sources of German Industrial Power*, Cambridge: Cambridge University Press.

Hibino, B. (1997), 'The transmission of work systems: A comparison of US and Japan auto's human resource management practices in Mexico', in R. Whitley and P.H. Kristensen (eds), *Governance at Work: The Social Regulation of Economic Relations*, Oxford: Oxford University Press, pp. 158–70.

Hill, S. (1981), *Competition and Control at Work*, Cambridge, MA: MIT Press.

Hirao, S. (2001), 'Egalitarian values stifle creativity: Researcher', *The Japan Times Online*, http://www.japantimes.co.jp/cgi-bin/getarticle.pl5? nn200101128a3.htm, 28 January.

Hirst, P. and J. Zeitlin (1989), *Reversing Industrial Decline? Industrial Structure and Policy in Britain and Her Competitors*, Oxford: Berg Publishers Limited.

Hislop, D., Newell, S., Scarborough, H. and J. Swan (1998), 'Innovation and networks: Linking diffusion and implementation', *International Journal of Innovation Management*, **1** (4): 427–48.

Ho, S. (1993), 'Transplanting Japanese management techniques', *Long Range Planning*, **26** (4): 81–9.

Hollingsworth, J.R. and R. Boyer (1997), *Contemporary Capitalism: The Embeddedness of Institutions*, Cambridge: Cambridge University Press.

Huberman, A.M. and M.B. Miles (1998), 'Data management and analysis methods', in N.K. Denzin and Y.S. Lincoln (eds), *Collecting and Interpreting Qualitative Materials*, Thousand Oaks, CA: Sage Publications, pp. 179–210.

Hull, F.M., Hage, J. and K. Azumi (1985), 'R&D management strategies: America versus Japan', *IEEE Transactions on Engineering Management*, **32** (2): 78–83.

Hyman, R. (2001), 'Trade union research and cross-national comparison', *European Journal of Industrial Relations*, **7** (2): 203–32.

Imai, M. (1986), *Kaizen: The Key to Japan's Competitive Success*, New York: McGraw-Hill Publishing Company.

Inkpen, A.C. and A. Dinur (1998), 'Knowledge management processes and international joint ventures', *Organization Science*, **9** (4): 452–68.

Invest in Britain Bureau (1995), *Japanese Manufacturing Companies in the UK*, 3 October, London: Department of Trade and Industry Publication.

Invest in Britain Bureau (1999), *Invest in Britain*, London: Department of Trade and Industry.

Invest.UK (2000), *Investment Bulletin*, Summer, http://www.invest.uk.com.

Jaegar, A.M. (1983), 'The transfer of organizational culture overseas: An approach to control in the multinational corporation', *Journal of International Business Studies*, **15**: 91–114.

Jeremy, D.J. (1981), *Transatlantic Industrial Revolution*, Oxford: Blackwell.

Karnøe, P. (1995), 'Institutional interpretations and explanations of differences in American and Danish approaches to innovation', in W.R. Scott and S. Christensen (eds), *The Institutional Construction of Organizations*, Thousand Oaks, CA: Sage Publications Inc., pp. 243–76.

Karnøe, P. and C. Nygaard (1999), 'Bringing social action and situated rationality back in', *International Studies of Management and Organization*, **29** (2): 78–93.

Kedia, B. and R. Bhagat (1988), 'Cultural constraints on transfer of technology across nations: Implications for research in international and comparative management', *Academy of Management Review*, **13** (4): 559–71.

Kenney, M. and R. Florida (1993), *Beyond Mass Production: The Japanese System and Its Transfer to the US*, New York: Oxford University Press.

Kenney, M. and R. Florida (1995), 'The transfer of Japanese management styles in two US transplant industries: Autos and electronics', *Journal of Management Studies*, **32** (6): 789–802.

Kester, W.C. (1996), 'American and Japanese corporate governance: Convergence to best practice?', in S. Berger and R. Dore (eds), *National Diversity and Global Capitalism*, Ithaca: Cornell University Press, pp. 107–37.

Kogut, B. and U. Zander (1992), 'Knowledge of the firm, combinative capabilities and the replication of technology', *Organization Science*, **3** (3): 383–97.

Kogut, B. and U. Zander (1993), 'Knowledge of the firm and the evolutionary theory of the multinational corporation', *Journal of International Business Studies*, **24**: 625–45.

Koike, K. (1993), 'Nihon kigyo to chiteki jukuren (Japanese firms and knowledge proficiency)', in T. Kagono, N. Itami and M. Ito (eds), *Nihon no Kigyo System (Japanese Management System)*, **3**, Tokyo: Yuhikaku, pp. 53–76.

Kostova, T. (1999), 'Transnational transfer of strategic organizational practices: A contextual perspective', *Academy of Management Review*, **24** (2): 308–24.

Kubo, I. and A. Saka (2002), 'An inquiry into the motivations of knowledge workers in the Japanese financial industry', *Journal of Knowledge Management*, **6** (3): 262–71.

Lahit, R.K. and M.M. Beyerlein (2000), 'Knowledge transfer and management consulting: A look at the firm', *Business Horizons*, **43** (1): 65–74.

Lam, A. (1998), 'Tacit knowledge, organizational learning and innovation: A societal perspective', *DRUID Working Paper*, No. 98–22, Danish Research Unit for Industrial Dynamics, Aolborg.

Lam, A. (2000), 'Tacit knowledge, organizational learning and societal institutions: An integrated framework', *Organization Studies*, **21** (3): 488–513.

Lane, C. (1996), 'The social constitution of supplier relations in Britain and Germany: An institutionalist analysis', in R. Whitley and P.H.

Kristensen (eds), *The Changing European Firm: Limits to Convergence*, London: Routledge, pp. 271–304.

Lane, C. and R. Bachman (1997), 'Co-operation in inter-firm relations in Britain and Germany: The role of social institutions', *British Journal of Sociology*, **48** (2): 226–54.

Lanzara, G.F. and G. Patriotta (2000), 'Technology and the courtroom: An inquiry into knowledge making', Paper presented at the *Knowledge Management: Concepts and Controversies Conference*, 10–11 February, University of Warwick, Coventry.

Lave, J. (1993), 'The practice of learning', in S. Chaiklin and J. Lave (eds), *Understanding Practice: Perspectives on Activity and Context*, Cambridge: Cambridge University Press, pp. 3–32.

Lazonick, W. (1998). 'Organizational learning and international competition', in J. Michie and J. Grieve Smith (eds), *Globalization, Growth and Governance*, Oxford: Oxford University Press, pp. 204–38.

Leonard-Barton, D. (1995), *Wellsprings of Knowledge: Building and Sustaining the Sources of Innovation*, Boston: Harvard Business School Press.

Lewchuk, W. (1992), 'Fordist technology and Britain: The diffusion of labour speed-up', in D.J. Jeremy (ed.), *The Transfer of International Technology; Europe, Japan and the USA in the Twentieth Century*, Aldershot: Edward Elgar, pp. 7–32.

Liker, J.K., Fruin, W.M. and P.S. Adler (1999), *Remade in America: Transplanting and Transforming Japanese Management Systems*, New York: Oxford University Press.

Lillrank, P. (1995), 'The transfer of management innovations from Japan', *Organization Studies*, **16** (6): 971–89.

Lincoln, J.R. and A.L. Kalleberg (1985), 'Work organization and workforce commitment: A study of plants and employees in the US and Japan', *American Sociological Review*, **50**: 738–60.

Lincoln, J.R. and A.L. Kalleberg (1990), *Culture, Control and Commitment: A Study of Work Organization and Work Attitudes in the United States and Japan*, Cambridge: Cambridge University Press.

Loveridge, R. (1987), 'Social accommodations and technological transformations – The case of gender', in G. Lee and R. Loveridge (eds), *The Manufacture of Disadvantage: Stigma and Social Change*. Milton Keynes: Open University Press, pp. 176–97.

Loveridge, R. (1996), 'Putting nationalism back into national business systems: The ideological and institutional context of global competition', *Research Paper*, Aston University, Birmingham.

Loveridge, R. (1998), 'Review of *The Changing European Firm – Limits to Convergence*', by R. Whitley and P.H. Kristensen (eds), *Organization Studies*, **19** (6): 1049–53.

Loveridge, R. and F. Mueller (2000), 'Flagships, flotillas and corvettes: Corporate actors, national business systems and sectoral dynamics in telecommunications', in S. Quack, G. Morgan and R. Whitley (eds), *National Capitalisms, Global Competition and Economic Performance*, Amsterdam: John Benjamins Publishing Company, pp. 213–35.

Lynskey, M.J. (1999), 'The transfer of resources and competencies for developing technologies capabilities – The case of Fujitsu-ICL', *Technology Analysis and Strategic Management*, **11** (3): 317–36.

MacDuffie, J. (1995), 'Human resource bundles and manufacturing performance: Organizational logic and flexible production systems in the world auto industry', *Industrial and Labour Relations Review*, **48** (2): 197–221.

Mair, A. (1998), 'Internationalization at Honda: Transfer and adaptation of management systems', *Employee Relations*, **20** (3): 285–302.

Makino, S. and A. Delios (1996), 'Local knowledge transfer and performance: Implications for alliance formation in Asia', *Journal of International Business Studies*, **27** (5): 905–27.

March, J.G. and J.P. Olsen (1984), 'The new institutionalism: Organizational factors in political life', *American Political Science Review*, **78** (3): 734–49.

Marini, M.M. (1992), 'The role of models of purposive action in sociology', in J.S. Coleman and T.J. Fararo (eds), *Rational Choice Theory: Advocacy and Critique*, Newbury Park: Sage Publications Inc., pp. 21–48.

Marshall, C. and G.B. Rossman (1995), *Designing Qualitative Research*, Second edition, Thousand Oaks, CA: Sage Publications.

Marshall, N. and J. Sapsed (2000), 'The limits of disembodied knowledge: Challenges of inter-project learning in the production of complex products and systems', Paper presented at the *Knowledge Management: Concepts and Controversies Conference*, 10–11 February, University of Warwick, Coventry.

Martinex, J.I. and J.C. Jarillo (1989), 'The evolution of research on co-ordination mechanisms in multinational corporations', *Journal of International Business Studies*, **20** (3): 489–514.

Marton, K. (1986), *Multinationals, Technology, and Industrialization*, Lexington: Heath.

Mathieu, J. and D. Zajac (1990), 'A review and meta-analysis of the antecedents, correlates and consequences of organizational commitment', *Psychological Bulletin*, **108**: 171–94.

Maurice, M., Sellier, F. and J.-J. Silvestre (1986), *The Social Foundations of Industrial Power: A Comparison of France and Germany*, translated by Arthur Goldhammer, Cambridge, MA: MIT Press.

Maurice, M., Sorge, A. and M. Warner (1980), 'Societal differences in organizing manufacturing units: A comparison of France, West Germany, and Great Britain', *Organization Studies*, **1** (1): 59–86.

McKenna, E. (1994), *Business Psychology and Organizational Behaviour: A Students' Handbook,* Hove: Psychology Press.

McMillan, C.J. (1996), *The Japanese Industrial System*, Third edition, Berlin: Walter de Gruyter.

Miles, R.E. and C.C. Snow (1978), *Organizational Structure, Strategy and Process*, New York: McGraw-Hill.

Mill, J.S. (1974), *A System of Logic Ratiocinative and Inductive: Being a Connected View of the Principles of Evidence and the Methods of Scientific Investigation,* Toronto: University of Toronto Press.

Morgan, G., Kelly, W., Sharpe, D.R. and R. Whitley (2000a), 'Control in global corporations', Paper presented at the *Labour Process Conference*, April, University of Strathclyde.

Morgan, G., Kelly, W., Sharpe, D.R. and R. Whitley (2000b), 'Multi-nationals as organizations', Paper presented at the *16th EGOS Colloquium*, 2–4 July, Helsinki School of Economics and Business Administration, Helsinki, Finland.

Morris, J. (1988), 'The who, why and where of Japanese manufacturing investment in the UK', *Industrial Relations Journal*, **19** (1): 31–40.

Morris, J. and B. Wilkinson (1995), 'The transfer of Japanese management to alien institutional environment', *Journal of Management Studies*, Special Issue, **32** (36): 719–30.

Mowery, D., Oxley, J. and B. Silverman (1996), 'Strategic alliances and inter-firm knowledge transfer', *Strategic Management Journal*, **17**, Winter Special Issue: 77–91.

Mueller, F. and R. Loveridge (1997), 'Institutional, sectoral and corporate dynamics in the creation of global supply chains', in R. Whitley and P.H. Kristensen (eds), *Governance at Work: The Social Regulation of Economic Relations*, Oxford: Oxford University Press, pp. 140–57.

Murata, K. and A. Harrison (1991), *How to Make Japanese Management Methods Work in the West*, Aldershot: Gower Publishing.

Nelson, R.R. and S.G. Winter (1982), *An Evolutionary Theory of Economic Change*. Cambridge, MA: Harvard University Press.

News and Notes (1999), 'Japanese manufacturers in Europe', *Euro-Japanese Journal*, **5** (2): 58–63.

Nonaka, I. and H. Takeuchi (1995), *The Knowledge-Creating Company: How Japanese Companies Create the Dynamics of Innovation*, New York: Oxford University Press.

Nonaka, I. and J.K. Johansson (1985), 'Japanese management: What about the "hard" skills?', *Academy of Management Review*, **10** (2): 181–91.

Norton, J.A. and F.M. Bass (1987), 'A diffusion theory model of adoption and substitution for successive generations of high-technology products', *Management Science*, **33**: 1069–86.

Office for National Statistics (1999), Unpublished data on level of industrial dispute in the West Midlands.

Ohtani, N., Duke, S. and S. Ohtani (1997), *Japanese Design and Development*, Aldershot: Gower Publishing Limited.

Oliver, N. and B. Wilkinson, (1992), *The Japanization of British Industry: New Developments in the 1990s*, Oxford: Blackwell Publishers.

Oliver, N., Delbridge, R., Jones, D. and J. Lowe (1994), 'World class manufacturing: Further evidence in the lean production debate', *British Journal of Management*, **5**: 53–63.

Orrù, M. (1997), 'Institutional co-operation in Japanese and German capitalism', in M. Orrù, N.W. Biggart and G.G. Hamilton (eds), *The Economic Organization of East Asian Capitalism*, Thousand Oaks, CA: Sage Publications, pp. 311–39.

Orrù, M., Biggart, N.W. and G.G. Hamilton (1991), 'Organizational isomorphism in East Asia', in W.W. Powell and P.J. DiMaggio (eds), *The New Institutionalism in Organizational Analysis*, Chicago: The University of Chicago Press, pp. 361–89.

Pascale, R.T. and A.G. Athos (1986), *The Art of Japanese Management*, London: Penguin Books Ltd.

Patel, P. and K. Pavitt (1997), 'The technological competencies of the world's largest firms: Complex and path-dependent, but not much variety', *Research Policy*, **26**: 141–56.

Pavitt, K. (1984), 'Sectoral patterns of technological change: Towards a taxonomy and a theory', *Research Policy*, **13**: 343–73.

Penrose, E.T. (1959), *The Theory of the Growth of the Firm*, Oxford: Basil Blackwell.

Platt, J. (1988), 'What can case studies do?', in R.G. Burgess (ed.), *Studies in Qualitative Methodology: A Research Annual, Conducting Qualitative Research*, 1, London: JAI Press, pp. 1–23.

Polanyi, M. (1966), *The Tacit Dimension*, London: Routledge and Kegan Paul.

Porter, M.E. (1990), *The Competitive Advantage of Nations*, New York: Free Press.

Porter, M.E., Takeuchi, H. and M. Sakakibara (2000), *Can Japan Compete?* Basingstoke: Macmillan Press Ltd.

Powell, W.W. (1991), 'Expanding the scope of institutional analysis', in W.W. Powell and P.J. DiMaggio (eds), *The New Institutionalism in Organizational Analysis*, Chicago: The University of Chicago Press, pp. 183–203.

Prahalad, C. and G. Hamel (1990), 'The core competence of the corporation', *Harvard Business Review*, **May–June**: 79–91.

Prusak, L. (1997), *Knowledge in Organizations*, Boston: Butterworth-Heinemann.

Raymond, M. (1996), *Research Made Simple: A Handbook for Social Workers*, Thousand Oaks, CA: Sage Publications Inc.

Reitsperger, W. (1986), 'British employees: Responding to Japanese philosophies', *Journal of Management Studies*, **23** (5): 563–86.

Richter, F.-J. and K. Vettel (1995), 'Successful joint ventures in Japan: Transferring knowledge through organizational learning', *Long Range Planning*, **28** (3): 37–45.

Robertson, M. (1999), *Sustaining Knowledge Creation Within Knowledge Intensive Firms*, Unpublished PhD dissertation, University of Warwick.

Rogers, E.M. (1983), *Diffusion of Innovations*, Third edition, New York: Free Press.

Rose, R. (1991), 'Comparing forms of comparative analysis', *Political Studies*, **39**: 446–62.

Rosenzweig, P.M. and N. Nohria (1994), 'Influences on human resource management practices in multinational corporations', *Journal of International Business Studies*, **Second quarter**: 229–51.

Rowlinson, M. (1997), *Organizations and Institutions*, Basingstoke: Macmillan Press Ltd.

Sahlin-Andersson, K. (1996), 'Imitating by editing success: The construction of organization fields', in B. Czarniawska and G. Sevón (eds), *Translating Organizational Change*, Berlin: Walter de Gruyter, pp. 69–92.

Sako, M. (1992), *Prices, Quality and Trust: Inter-Firm Relations in Britain and Japan*, Cambridge: Cambridge University Press.

Sako, M. (1997), 'Introduction: Forces for homogeneity and diversity in the Japanese industrial relations system', in M. Sako and H. Sato (eds), *Japanese Labour and Management in Transition: Diversity, Flexibility and Participation,* London: Routledge, pp. 1–24.

Sako, M. and H. Sato (1997), *Japanese Labour and Management in Transition*, London: Routledge.

Scarbrough, H. (1995), 'Blackboxes, hostages and prisoners', *Organization Studies*, **16** (6): 991–1019.

Scarbrough, H. and M. Corbett (1992), *Technology and Organization*, London: Routledge.

Scarbrough, H. and J. Swan (1999), *Case Studies in Knowledge Management*, London: Institute of Personnel and Development.

Scarbrough, H. and M. Terry (1998), 'Forget Japan: The very British response to lean production', *Employee Relations*, **20** (3): 224–36.

Scarbrough, H., Swan, J.A. and J. Preston (1998), *Knowledge Management and the Learning Organization: The IPD Report*, London: Institute of Personnel Development.

Schatzman, L. and A.L. Strauss (1973), *Field Research: Strategies for a Natural Sociology*, Englewood Cliffs: Prentice-Hall.

Selznick, P. (1957), *Leadership in Administration: A Sociological Interpretation*, New York: Harper & Row.

Senker, J. (1995), 'Tacit knowledge and models of innovation', *Industrial and Corporate Change*, **4** (2): 425–47.

Sevón, G. (1996), 'Organizational imitation in identity transformation', in B. Czarniawska and G. Sevón (eds), *Translating Organizational Change*, Berlin: Walter de Gruyter, pp. 49–67.

Sewell, G. and B. Wilkinson (1992), '"Someone to watch over me": Surveillance, discipline and the just-in-time labour process', *Sociology*, **26** (2): 271–89.

Sharpe, D.R. (1997), 'Compromise solutions: A Japanese multinational comes to the UK', in R. Whitley and P.H. Kristensen (eds), *Governance at Work: The Social Regulation of Economic Relations*, Oxford: Oxford University Press, pp. 171–89.

Sharpe, D.R. (1998), *Shop Floor Practices Under Changing Forms of Managerial Control: A Comparative Ethnographic Study*, Unpublished PhD dissertation, University of Manchester.

Sharpe D.R. (1999), 'Globalization and change: An in-depth case study of processes of organizational continuity and change within a Japanese Multinational in the UK', Paper presented at the *European Summer Research Institutes (ESRI) Workshop on Comparative Study of Economic Organization*, Copenhagen Business School, Denmark, 24–28 September.

Sharpe, D.R. (2001), 'Globalization and change: Organizational continuity and change within a Japanese multinational in the UK', in G. Morgan, P.H. Kristensen and R. Whitley (eds), *The Multinational Firm: Organizing Across Institutional and National Divides*, Oxford: Oxford University Press, pp. 196–221.

Sharpe, D.R., Kelly, W., Morgan, G. and R. Whitley (2000), 'The global manager? Japanese expatriate managers – Managing over distance and time', Paper presented at the *Academy of Management Conference*, 4–9 August, Toronto, Canada.

Sierra, M.C. de la (1995), *Managing Global Alliances: Key Steps for Successful Collaboration*, Wokingham: Addison-Wesley Publishing Company.

Skorstad, E. (1994), 'Lean production, conditions of work and worker commitment', *Economic and Industrial Democracy*, **15**: 429–55.

Slappendel, C. (1996), 'Perspectives on innovation in organizations', *Organization Studies*, **17** (1): 107–29.

Smith, C. and T. Elger (1998), 'Greenfields and "wildebeests": Management strategies and labour turnover in Japanese firms in Telford', *Employee Relations*, **20** (3): 271–84.

Sorge, A. (1989), 'An essay on technical change: Its dimensions and social and strategic context', *Organization Studies*, **10** (1): 23–44.

Sorge, A. (1991), 'Strategic fit and the societal effect: Interpreting cross-national comparisons of technology, organization and human resources', *Organization Studies*, **12** (2): 161–90.

Sorge, A. (1996), 'Societal effects in cross-national organization studies: Conceptualization diversity in actors and systems', in R. Whitley and P.H. Kristensen (eds), *The Changing European Firm*, London: Routledge, pp. 67–86.

Spender, J.C. (1996), 'Making knowledge the basis of a dynamic theory of the firm', *Strategic Management Journal*, **16**, Special Issue: 45–62.

Stewart, P. (1998), 'Out of chaos comes order: From Japanization to lean production: A critical commentary', *Employee Relations*, **20** (3): 213–23.

Streeck, W. (1996), 'Lean production in the German automobile industry: A test case for convergence theory', in S. Berger and R. Dore (eds), *National Diversity and Global Capitalism*, New York: Cornell University Press, pp. 138–70.

Streeck, W. (1997), 'German capitalism: Does it exist? Can it survive?', in C. Crouch and W. Streeck (eds), *Political Economy of Modern Capitalism*, London: Sage, pp. 33–54.

Stringer, E.T. (1996), *Action Research: A Handbook for Practitioners*, Thousand Oaks: Sage Publications.

Sullivan, J., Peterson, R.B., Kameda, N. and J. Shimada (1981), 'The relationship between conflict resolution approaches and trust: A cross-cultural study', *Academy of Management Journal*, **24** (4): 803–15.

Suzuki, Y. (1980), *Money and Banking in Contemporary Japan*, New Haven: Yale University Press.

Swan, J.A. (1999), 'Introduction', in H. Scarbrough and J. Swan (eds), *Case Studies in Knowledge Management*, London: Institute of Personnel and Development, pp. 1–12.

Swan, J.A. and P. Clark (1992), 'Organizational decision-making in the appropriation of technological innovation: Cognitive and political dimensions', *European Work and Organizational Psychologist*, **2** (2): 103–27.

Swan, J.A., Newell, S. and M. Robertson (1999), 'Central agencies in the diffusion and design of technology: A comparison of the UK and Sweden', *Organization Studies*, **20** (6): 905–31.

Szulanski, G. (1996), 'Exploring internal stickiness: Impediments to the transfer of best practice within the firm', *Strategic Management Journal*, **17**, Winter Special Issue: 27–43.

Taggart, J. (1998), 'Locating international pharmaceutical R&D subsidiaries: Between-countries and within-countries determinants', in G. Hooley, R. Loveridge and D. Wilson (eds), *Internationalization: Process, Context and Markets*, Basingstoke: Macmillan Press Ltd., pp. 56–77.

Takeuchi, H. (1981), 'Productivity: Learning from the Japanese', *California Management Review*, **4**: 5–19.

Takeuchi, H. (1998), 'Beyond knowledge management, lessons from Japan', http://www.sveiby.com/articles/LessonsJapan.htm, 10 June.

Tampoe, M. (1993), 'Motivating knowledge workers – The challenge for the 1990s', *Long Range Planning*, **26** (3): 49–55.

Taylor, B., Elger, T. and P. Fairbrother (1994), 'Transplants and emulators: The fate of the Japanese model in British electronics', in T. Elger and C. Smith (eds), *Global Japanization? The Transnational Transformation of the Labour Process*, London: Routledge, pp. 196–225.

Teece, D. and G. Pisano (1994), 'The dynamic capabilities of firms: An introduction', *Industrial and Corporate Change*, **3**: 537–56.

Thomas, R.J. (1994), *What Machines Can't Do: Politics and Technology in the Industrial Enterprise*, Berkeley: University of California Press.

Tolbert, P.S. and L.G. Zucker (1983), 'Institutional sources of change in the formal structure of organizations: The diffusion of civil service reform, 1880–1935', *Administrative Science Quarterly*, **28** (1): 22–39.

Tolich, M., Kenney, M. and N. Biggart (1999), 'Managing the managers: Japanese management strategies in the USA', *Journal of Management Studies*, **36** (5): 587–607.

Tsang, E.W.K. (2001), 'Managerial learning in foreign-invested enterprises of China', *Management International Review*, **41**: 29–51.

Tsoukas, H. (1996), 'The firm as a distributed knowledge system: A constructionist approach', *Strategic Management Journal*, **17**, Winter Special Issue: 1–25.

Tsui-Auch, L.S. (2001), 'Learning in global and local networks: Experience of Chinese firms in Hong Kong, Singapore and Taiwan' in M. Dierkes, A. Berthoin Antal, J. Child and I. Nonaka (eds), *Handbook of Organizational Learning and Knowledge*, Oxford: Oxford University Press, pp. 716–32.

Turnbull, P. and R. Delbridge (1994), 'Making sense of Japanization: A review of the British experience', *International Journal of Employment Studies*, **2** (2): 343–65.

Tushman, M.L. and T.J. Scanlan (1981), 'Boundary spanning individuals: Their role in information transfer and their antecedents', *Academy of Management Journal*, **24**: 289–305.

Warner, M. (1994), 'Japanese culture, Western management: Taylorism and human resources in Japan', *Organization Studies*, **15** (4): 509–33.

Westney, D.E. (1987), *Imitation and Innovation: The Transfer of Western Organizational Patterns to Meiji Japan*, Cambridge, MA: Harvard University Press.

Westney, D.E. (1993), 'Institutionalization theory and the multinational corporation', in S. Ghoshal and D.E. Westney (eds), *Organization Theory and the Multinational Corporation*, New York: St. Martin's Press, pp. 53–76.

Westney, D.E. (1999), 'Organization theory perspectives on the cross-border transfer of organizational patterns', in J.K. Liker, W.M. Fruin and P.S. Adler (eds), *Remade in America: Transplanting and Trans-forming Japanese Management Systems*, New York: Oxford University Press, pp. 385–408.

White, M.R. and M. Trevor (1983), *Under Japanese Management*, London: Heinemann.

Whitley, R. (1992), *Business Systems in East Asia: Firms, Markets and Societies*, London: Sage Publications.

Whitley, R. (1996), 'The social construction of economic actors: Institutions and types of firm in Europe and other market economies', in R.D. Whitley and P.H. Kristensen (eds), *The Changing European Firm: Limits to Convergence*, London: Routledge, pp. 39–66.

Whitley, R. (1997), 'The social regulation of work systems: Institutions, interest groups and varieties of work organization in capitalist societies', in R.D. Whitley and P.H. Kristensen (eds), *Governance at Work: The Social Regulation of Economic Relations*, Oxford: Oxford University Press, pp. 227–60.

Whitley, R. (1999a), 'Competing logics and units of analysis in the comparative study of economic organization: The comparative-business-systems framework in perspective', *International Studies of Management and Organization*, **29** (2): 113–26.

Whitley, R. (1999b), *Divergent Capitalisms: The Social Structuring and Change of Business Systems*, Oxford: Oxford University Press.

Whitley, R. (1999c), 'How and why are international firms different? The consequences of cross-border managerial coordination for firm characteristics and behaviour', Paper presented at the *15th EGOS Colloquium*, 4–6 July, University of Warwick, Coventry.

Whitley, R. (2000a), 'Changing regulatory regimes and the management of international business transactions', Paper presented at the *ESRI Workshop on Forms of Transnational Governance and Paths of Economic Development*, 16–19 September, Lisbon, Portugal.

Whitley, R. (2000b), 'The institutional structuring of innovation strategies:

Business systems, firm types and patterns of technical change in different market economies', *Organization Studies*, Special Issue on the institutional dynamics of innovation systems, **21** (5): 855–86.

Wilkinson, B. and N. Oliver (1992), 'Human resource management in Japanese manufacturing companies in the UK and USA', in B. Towers (ed.), *The Handbook of Human Resource Management*, Oxford: Blackwell, pp. 50–68.

Williams, K., Haslam, C., Adcroft, A. and S. Johal (1992), 'Against lean production', *Economy and Society*, **August**: 321–54.

Williamson, O.E. (1985), *The Economic Institutions of Capitalism: Markets, Hierarchies and Relational Contracting*, New York: The Free Press.

Wilms, W.W., Alan, J.H. and D.M. Zell (1994), 'Cultural transformation at NUMMI', *Sloan Management Review*, **36** (1): 99–113.

Wolfe, R.A. (1994), 'Organizational innovation: Review, critique and suggested research directions', *Journal of Management Studies*, **31**: 405–31.

Womack, J.P., Jones, D.T. and D. Roos (1990), *The Machine That Changed the World*, New York: Macmillan.

Worsley, P. (1982), *Marx and Marxism*, Chichester: Ellis Horwood Ltd.

Yin, R.K. (1994), *Case Study Research: Design and Methods*, Second edition, Thousand Oaks: Sage Publications.

Yoshimura, N. and P. Anderson (1997), *Inside the Kaisha: Demystifying Japanese Business Behaviour*, Boston: Harvard Business School Press.

Yoshino, M. (1968), *Japan's Managerial System: Tradition and Innovation*, Cambridge, MA: MIT Press.

Zysman, J. (1983), *Governments, Markets and Growth*, Ithaca: Cornell University Press.

Index